The **IMPACT** *of Europe in 1992 on West Africa*

Edited by Olesegun Obasanjo and Hans d'Orville

Foreword by Lord Callaghan of Cardiff

CRANE RUSSAK
A Member of the Taylor & Francis Group
New York · Bristol, PA · Washington, DC · London

USA	Publishing Office:	Taylor & Francis New York Inc. 79 Madison Ave., New York, NY 10016-7892
	Sales Office:	Taylor & Francis Inc. 1900 Frost Road, Bristol, PA 19007-1598
UK		Taylor & Francis Ltd. 4 John St., London WC1N 2ET

The Impact of Europe in 1992 on West Africa

First published 1990
Printed in the United States of America

Library of Congress Cataloging in Publication Data

The Impact of Europe in 1992 on West Africa / edited by Olusegun Obasanjo
  and Hans d'Orville.
      p.   cm.
  Papers from a conference held in Brussels, Belgium, Apr. 21–23, 1989.
  ISBN 0-8448-1672-8
  1. Africa, West—Foreign economic relations—European Economic
Community countries—Congresses.   2. European Economic Community
countries—Foreign economic relations—Africa, West—Congresses.
3. Economic Community of West African States—Congresses.
4. Africa, West—Economic integration—Congresses.   5. Europe 1992—
Congresses.   6. Economic assistance, European—Africa, West—
Congresses.   I. Obasanjo, Olusegun.   II. Orville, Hans d', 1949–.
HF1615.5.Z4E865   1990
337.406—dc20   90-38669
                                                                    CIP

Contents

Foreword

1992 is just over the horizon, and this book drawn up under the Chairman-ship of General Obasanjo, former Head of State of Nigeria, comes as a timely reminder to Europeans and to others in the industrialized world of the adverse consequences which will befall some of the very poorest West African countries unless Europe's trade, aid and investment policies take full and urgent account of the desperate poverty of Africa's people. Unfortunately, there has been a decline of interest in recent years in Africa and the third world and this is likely to be accelerated by the present attention being given to the problems of renewing and reviving the economies and political structures of Eastern Europe. Western European private investment is likely to find the East European market more attractive than African, with that continent's heavy indebtedness (over 40% of West Africa's exports go to pay for debt service), and the poverty of the rural population which bears the brunt of the burden.

Africa is truly a continent in continuing crisis, for whose people there will be no escape until the outflow of resources can be stemmed, debt remitted, and higher prices secured for its major cash crops such as coffee and cocoa whose prices have plummetted.

To deepen the difficulties, although the European Community is West Africa's major trading partner, both the volume and the value of the exports of the 16 members of the Economic Community of West African States (ECOWAS) is even now stagnating or falling.

European and African skeptics point to corrupt authorities, slipshod contractors and incompetent bureaucracies as causes of the recent decline in foreign private investment, to which the world bank has added its own alarm at "the process of political decline." ECOWAS was constituted 15 years ago under Nigerian leadership to do something for West Africa on the lines of the European Communities achievements. But the conditions were very different even before it began, and it has not been a success nor has it left any real mark.

Yet despite all this, the tone of the contributors, including Africans, to "Europe in 1992 and the implications for West Africa" is refreshing indeed. The evident self-criticism pinpointing reasons for the failure of ECOWAS, coupled with real determination to better the lot of the African countries, be it at the national, sub-regional or regional level, could mark a new beginning in the economic and social fortunes of West Africa.

Many Africans recognize that only they can solve some of the problems outlined in this report. But it is equally true that we cannot succeed without outside help and it is Europe which for historical and other reasons should provide assistance, encouragement and even possibly a model.

The completion of the Single European Market by the end of 1992 has raised fears and misgivings about the emergence of a "fortress Europe." I do not believe that these fears will turn out to be true, but if the challenge of a more closely integrated Europe is to be met, West Africa must organize itself to speak on more equal terms. There are difficulties. Most ECOWAS countries possess similar economies, export similar primary products and import similar manufactures. They exchange relatively little between themselves. It is clear that an effective larger entity such as ECOWAS which would foster coordination and cooperation between them would be able to take advantage of scale to increase the bargaining power of all its members.

That is the message of the Africa Leadership Forum, and what applies to West Africa also applies to the rest of sub-Saharan Africa. The chairman of the conference, General Obasanjo, has consistently shown that he understands what is required and also knows the European dimension. I trust that he will be able successfully to follow up the conclusions of the conference and devise a plan that will revive ECOWAS and arouse the people and politicians of his Continent to take the necessary action.

Finally, I must repeat that it is the responsibility of the industrialized world, in particular of the countries of the European Community, to support such efforts by providing vital financial resources, by further remission of debt and other public and private investment, training human resources, opening up trade barriers, and making technology available. Without much greater European and other assistance in all these fields that has been made available hitherto, no political structures, no economic coordination, no amount of effort by the African countries themselves can hope to succeed. We in the countries of the North, should without delay, move to fulfill our part in the international compact that will encourage and support the people of Africa and their leaders to move towards a more hopeful and better future.

Lord Callaghan of Cardiff
Prime Minister of the United Kingdom
1976–79

Preface

The principal theme of the meeting on the impact of Europe in 1992 on West Africa, held in Brussels, Belgium, 21–23 April 1989, was to assess the impact on West Africa of the completion of the European Market in 1992. A second focus involved an examination of the reasons why economic integration had proceeded so slowly in light of the gathering momentum of progress toward economic integration among the 12 members of the European Economic Community (EEC).

The conference had to objectives: 1) to examine the tangible impact of the effects of the 1992 single European market on West Africa and, based thereon, to develop a plan of action for governments and the business community as to how best to adapt to the emerging situation; and 2) to deduce from the EEC experience a blueprint for steps required to move towards a more open and integrated market and more intensive cooperation in West Africa.

General Olusegun Obasanjo, chairman of the African Leadership Forum, opened the conference by describing the anxieties and uncertainties over the impact of completing the European market shared by the many countries—developed and undeveloped—that are Europe's trading partners. Despite general assurances by the European Commission that Europe after 1992 would not become an economic fortress with higher levels of protection but rather a more dynamic trading partner and continue to fulfill its international obligations, West Africa still feared that its trade with the Community, which remained a very large percentage of its total trade, its foreign investment—still stemming in large part from the EC, and its aid flows, of which the EC was the largest source, would be affected in unpredictable and possibly adverse ways.

A discussion memo specifically prepared for the conference made the following points:

- Completing the European market was an exercise in deregulation. All barriers to the free movement of goods, services, capital and persons would be removed if harmonized. It did not appear that monetary union among EC members would occur by 1992.
- EC member states remain the principal trading partners, foreign investors and sources of foreign aid for countries of West Africa.
- The completion of the common European market may not have a major impact on West African countries in the short run because they export mainly primary products to Europe and the regulations affecting those products are unlikely to change (except in a few cases, such as bananas). The long run impact is difficult to predict. A more rapidly growing EC will likely import more from its trade partners, including those in West Africa. It will probably also attract more investment, possibly reducing the amount of investment otherwise available for Africa. And eventually, West African countries will want to produce and export manufactured goods to the EC. The completion of the EC market could make the export of such goods to Europe more difficult if barriers to such imports rise or if competition within the EC results in lower cost production of manufactures by EC producers themselves.

A number of African participants emphasized these points:

- At present most African countries are involved in structural adjustment programs. These are painful and their outcome still uncertain. Additional uncertainties from changes within the EC made anxieties within African governments particularly acute.
- West Africans may not be able to exploit fully new opportunities for trade and investment arising from EC 92, given their weak bargaining position and past record of weak economic management.
- The long-run impact of EC 92 may be far more significant than any immediate impact, possibly making future exports of manufactured goods from West Africa to the EC more difficult and diverting investment that might have located in Africa to the EC.

A member of the European Commission reacted with the following:

- Europe will become truly one market in 1992. Monetary union, however, was not planned as part of that market by 1992.
- The effects of the move toward a single market are already evident in

the recent spurt in economic growth within the EC. That growth results in higher levels of imports, including from West Africa.

- European national preference systems with less-developed countries will change with the completion of the European market. But there will be no replacement of national quantitative restrictions with European quotas. European quantitative restrictions, such as the Multifiber Textile Agreement, should also be eliminated as soon as is possible.
- The EC must look for new ways of cooperation with developing countries, including within the Lome Agreement. An obvious opportunity involves private investment from EC countries to those developing countries with an interest in and willingness to explore new arrangements such as those that are being evolved with countries of Eastern Europe and elsewhere.

Other representatives of the European Commission made these points:

- Within the current and future Lomé agreements, there is no risk of having the European market closed in any way. Free access to the EC market will remain.
- Completion of the EC market will not lead to more protection. But existing quantitative restrictions by individual EC members on some nine commodities imported from member countries of the Lome Agreement would disappear.
- Standards and norms for goods and services sold in the EC will not be harmonized. Rather, standards and norms by one member state will be recognized and accepted by all others. Thus if an African export is acceptable in one market, it will be accepted in all EC markets.
- Private capital must remain important in Africa's future development. Where incentives are present and structural adjustment effective, private investment will flow. It is not inevitable that European capital will disengage from countries where conditions are not favorable. In regard to foreign aid, the European Development Fund (EDF) will not be diluted. Bilateral aid programs from EC member states will not be absorbed into the EDF.
- In regard to monetary union within the EC, there is movement forward but not with dramatic speed. Speculations about how the franc zone will be handled within a monetary union in the EC are premature. In any case, there is no reason even within a European monetary union, why franc zone countries wishing to maintain their links with Europe could not do so.

- Finally, EC aid is increasingly provided in support of structural adjustment in recipient countries. This aid is coordinated with, but not subordinated to similar aid from the World Bank and IMF.

A major proportion of the discussions was dedicated to considering the problems and prospects for economic integration in West Africa and specifically among the 16 members of the Economic Community of West African States. ECOWAS was established in 1975 with the objective of achieving economic integration among member states. By creating an integrated market of over 150 million people and the economies of scale necessary to support large-scale industrial production, it was expected that trade among member states would expand, investment would rise, and employment, income, and growth would increase.

It was observed that ECOWAS had yet to make good on its objectives of economic integration. As a result, intra-ECOWAS trade remains small. There are many reasons for this lack of progress, but the most surprising was the lack of political will in the region. It was time to make a new beginning on economic integration in West Africa. It was important for Africa's economic future, and important if Africa is to trade on terms of equality with its European and other trading partners. Without unity among Africans, they would have little leverage in international negotiations.

From the African side it was agreed that progress toward integration in ECOWAS was disappointing. ECOWAS had not succeeded in becoming a "people's project" or seen by the private sector in member countries (which is often foreign owned) as of benefit to them. These attitudes should be changed if ECOWAS is to succeed. Even though the economies of ECOWAS member states, in contrast to those of the EC, were not complementary, economic integration was still a real possibility and necessity. A high-level expert group could be set up, led by the chairman of the Africa Leadership Forum, to propose a strategy and measures for the revival of ECOWAS.

From the European side it was emphasized that regional integration must be taken more seriously by African countries. Otherwise, the delinking of African economies from the world economy, which was already apparent and of considerable concern, would likely continue. West Africans might wish to follow the European example and proceed step by step with small concrete steps at first rather than spend time and energy on grand schemes or argue about compensation for those countries suffering from the costs of integration. Political will and effective leadership would be important in making progress towards integration in West Africa as it was in Europe.

Participants from the business world underlined the importance of larger markets in Africa, the need for economies of scale to attract investors, and the importance of realizing the goals of ECOWAS.

A member of the EC Commission commented that economic cooperation was vital in Africa. The proliferation of regional organizations, however, might act as an obstacle to progress toward integration. It was important to avoid tackling large, visible projects as part of the process of integration. A step-by-step approach involving practical actions would be most effective. A regional approach to structural adjustment might make sense; at least, national structural adjustment programs should be compatible with regional cooperation.

General Obasanjo highlighted that it was still difficult to predict the impact of the completion of the European market on West Africa. It was clear, however, that Africa was being economically marginalized from the world economy. Regional integration was a means of halting the economic and political marginalization. A battle had been lost for regional cooperation within the framework of ECOWAS, but the war was still to be won. The Africa Leadership Forum was provided with a mandate to pursue in its further activities the question of future regional cooperation and integration within ECOWAS.

1

INTRODUCTION

Olusegun Obasanjo

At the end of 1992, the 12 member states of the European Community (EC) are resolved to complete the creation of a single European market by removing all remaining barriers to the free flow of goods and services within the EC. In other words, by the end of 1992, the European Common Market is supposed to become truly common. The European Commission itself has described this impending development as a "quiet revolution." Quiet it may be; revolution, it most assuredly is. An internal market of some 320 million people, with an annual GDP of $2.7 trillion, exports worth $680 billion, and imports of $708 billion—this, in brief outline, is the economic profile of the Europe of 1992. And as everyone recognizes, the completion of the single market will accentuate the EC's position as the world's leading trading bloc. How will this monumental development affect the 16 member countries of the Economic Community of West African States (ECOWAS)?

We are by no means alone in our interest in what Europe has embarked upon. Active interest in 1992 has become something of a universal phenomenon. It is the urgent subject for discussion wherever policymakers and opinion formers are gathered together. That interest is also usually shot through with anxiety. Japan and the United States, among Europe's major trading rivals, were first off the mark to make public their anxieties about the implications of 1992 for their trade with the EC. Their respective governments and corporate worlds have since started working out responses to this impending change in the structure of the world's trading system and the composition of its economic powers.

Among many of the African, Caribbean and Pacific States Group (ACP) group of countries linked to the European Community through the Lomé

Convention, interest in 1992 has been no less feverish. At the beginning of October 1988, the West India Committee and the Caribbean Community (CARICOM) secretariat organized a conference in London on the theme of "1992 and the Caribbean." The participants included a considerable number of Commonwealth Caribbean prime ministers, ministers, and senior officials as well as a distinguished group of over 200 people. And like this conference, the purpose of that meeting was to examine the implications of 1992 for the Caribbean region, to identify specific problem areas, and having formed a consensus on issues of common concern, to investigate in depth practical ways in which these problems could be tackled.

In a week's time, representatives of the Preferential Trade Area (PTA) will meet here to consider the implications of 1992 for the 15-member states of eastern and southern Africa. No doubt sooner or later the Pacific, too, will be astir with similar initiatives, if that is not already the case. This seminar is therefore part of this worldwide reaction to the impending completion of the single European market.

And this is as it should be. At the level of generalities, no one can doubt that the completion of the internal European market in 1992 will present considerable opportunities in addition to further strengthening the international trading system. All of us who trade with Europe will be selling to a single unified market of some 320 million consumers. We will be dealing with a uniform set of standards and procedures and not 12 different sets of requirements. For warrant, we have the word of the Commission itself and the burden of that assurance is that:

- The 1992 Europe will not be a fortress Europe but a partnership Europe.
- 1992 will be of benefit to Community and non-Community countries alike; and this is because the completion of the single market will also give a major boost to the Community, a boost that will have favorable repercussions both inside and outside the Community.
- 1992 will not mean protectionism because the Community has a fundamental stake in the existence of free and open international trade.
- The development of the Community's external economic policy in the run up to 1992 will take place in harmony with its existing international obligations, whether these be multilateral such as GATT or bilateral such as Lomé.

These are welcome assurances, but they do not go far enough and they certainly do not assuage all our anxieties. If they did, this conference would not take place. We in West Africa share with other ACP third parties a peculiar anxiety about 1992. The peculiarity of that anxiety arises from the fact that the present pattern of our exports to the EC is determined by market regulation with the individual members of the Community. And such regulation must inevitably be vulnerable in an exercise aiming at the demolition of barriers and restrictions on trade. But there are also other reservations about the Commission's assurances.

First, they are all general. They apply to all Europe's trading partners and to no one in particular. Second, there is no pretence that the repercussions of 1992 will be uniformly spread over all the Community's trading partners. In the nature of things, 1992 is bound to bestow affluence here and embarrassment there. How will the Europe of 1992 distribute its favors? In any case, even these general assurances will hold good only if, as the economists say, other things remain equal. The question is: What will remain "equal" after 1992 and what will not?

The answers to some of these questions will emerge only later and under the pressure and stimulus of the actual events as 1992 unfolds. But that is no reason for not raising them now. West Africa, like any other region, needs to be assured of a reasonable degree of predictability in its economic planning. Predictability is an indispensable key element of political activities and international relations in this age of global interdependence. And only by raising and answering the sorts of questions thrown up by the move to a single market in Europe will we be assured of a measure of provision into our economic future. This is one of our central expectations.

It is especially important that we in West Africa be as much as possible fully prepared for 1992. In spite of the vicissitudes of the commodity trade in recent years, the European Community remains West Africa's largest trading partner. No less than 70 percent of West Africa's principal exports—cocoa, timber, cotton, coffee, groundnuts, gold, and diamonds—goes to Europe. And it is from Europe that practically all West African countries derive the bulk of their imports of manufactured goods. In fact, so long-standing and so strong are the trading ties between the two regions that for virtually all West African countries, external trade is merely trade with Europe by another name. And related to this is the fact that a great deal of private investment in West Africa stems from countries of the European Community—principally Britain, France, and West Germany. We need to know as much as the clarity of the crystal ball will allow what 1992 will mean for these long-standing links and investment flows.

The ties born of trade and investment have been strengthened by those of aid. The European Community was the largest single source of foreign aid for 14 of the 16 member countries of ECOWAS in 1987. We would like to think that any increased prosperity accruing to the member countries in the Community as a result of 1992 will result in increased concessional aid flows to West Africa. Will we be right in so thinking?

In other respects too, the evolution of the European Community has direct implications for the future evolution of our own West African Community. Seven members of ECOWAS—Benin, Burkina Faso, Cote d'Ivoire, Mali, Niger, Senegal, and Togo—also form the West African Monetary Union. They are united in a single currency zone with a common central bank and a single common currency, the CFA franc, which is linked to the French franc. How will the matter of this overseas franc be handled? Will it be taken into the European Monetary System or will France help in the creation of a wider zone of convertibility within the framework of ECOWAS that will absorb the present seven of the West African Monetary Union?

By coincidence 1992 is also the year in which the monetary harmonization program agreed upon by ECOWAS heads of government at Abuja in July 1987 is due to come into effect. The program envisages a central bank, a common convertible West African currency, a common fiscal policy, a harmonized development strategy, and a liberalized trade policy. Currency harmonization is clearly indispensable to effective economic integration within West Africa. And in large measure our path to this objective has already been cleared by the fact that the economic recovery programs on which most member countries of ECOWAS have embarked have usually entailed substantial adjustments of exchange rates, thus bringing the exchange rates within the region into line with one another. There is an implementation committee mandate to negotiate this monetary harmonization within the region and we very much hope that the committee can count upon the support of European and other partners in the principal multilateral financial institutions in the prosecution of its mandate.

But beyond the immediate gains that we hope to be able to reap from 1992, we also look to the European example for inspiration in our efforts to build a thriving economic community in West Africa. ECOWAS was set up in May 1975 to pursue objectives very akin to those of the European Community. Like the EEC, it was to bring about economic union by stages through such measures as the:

- Elimination of customs duties.
- Abolition of administrative restrictions on trade.
- Establishment of a common customs tariff and a common commercial policy.
- Harmonization of economic and industrial policies.
- Harmonization of the monetary policies of member states.

Fourteen years later, virtually all these objectives have still to be made good. None of the member countries has come anywhere near meeting the tariff reduction deadlines that have already been revised and put back several times. The result is that there is still no preferential trade. And what exists by way of regional trade is minuscular—fluctuating around 4 percent of member countries' total exports. In any case the bulk of this is made up of oil and oil products. And there is no harmonization of industrial policies. As for the free movement of people, the least said about that the better. It is not just that ECOWAS has not much advanced beyond what it was in 1975, the fear is that it is now in danger of moving backward. President Jawara of the Gambia was only reflecting the true position in 1988 when he said, "We move from the problematic to what is in danger of becoming the unattainable."

We are all familiar with the reasons for the late evolution of ECOWAS:

- The fact that all member countries are producers and exporters of primary commodities and, therefore, leaving little margin for intraregional trade.
- The marked disparities in the levels of economic development as between the member states.
- The fact that for most ECOWAS countries, the major source of government revenue is tax, and consequently the reluctance to accept a reduction in tax revenues arising from a lowering of tariff barriers.
- To the structural problems have been added those of a contingent nature associated with the fall in commodity prices and the debt overhang.

And there is, of course, the legacy of colonial partition and all that implies in terms of economic integration. All these and more are difficulties enough to influence the pace of regional integration in West Africa. But, and this is the point to grasp, these factors also cut the other way and should have been precisely the reason impelling us to greater efforts at integration.

I agree that ultimately what is lacking to make the difference is the absence of the necessary political will. But frankly, this apparent lack of political will in the region is even more surprising.

- ECOWAS was not founded in a fit of absentmindedness on the part of West Africa's political leadership; and no country was dragooned into the Treat of Lagos of May 1975 and the subsequent protocols. Neither was it an external imposition on the region. The treaty together with its protocols remains an open covenant, openly arrived at and freely entered into.

- When the region's heads of government said they signed the treaty "in faith," they meant it. And it wasn't a blind faith either. They knew and appreciated full well the practical benefits of effective economic co-operation.
- And if they were alive to the benefits of economic integration, they could hardly have been ignorant of the dangers of continued economic fragmentation.
- It is often argued that in comparable contexts elsewhere in history, a perceived external threat has often served as the decisive factor to accelerate the pace of integration. But with deepening poverty and mounting external debt, to go no further, what more awesome threats do we in West Africa need to concentrate our minds wonderfully?

Clearly, the situation calls for a new beginning to the whole question of economic integration in West Africa. One fruitful approach is to make it a people's cause. If the pressure from below is perceptible and sufficiently credible, resistance from above will be to no avail. It is one of the ways in which we can rekindle our flickering West African flame from the European torch. No doubt there are other approaches that will emerge. The role of our intellectuals and other opinion formers in all this is self-evident.

One final thought. We are required to examine the implications of 1992 for West Africa; but we should encompasse the rest of sub-Saharan Africa, if not the whole of Africa. Why? First, being also commodity producers for the most part, much of what is true of West Africa also holds good for the other countries of sub-Saharan Africa. And second, as a result of Europe's decision to complete its internal market in 1992, African finance ministers decided at a meeting in Malawi in March 1988 to bring forward the date for the creation of an African Monetary Union. It is therefore not only West Africa that is preparing for 1992, it is the whole of Africa that is hurrying to meet the challenge of that year.

From this conference should stem a possible blueprint for the consideration of ECOWAS governments, business organizations, and other institutions of learning as they prepare for 1992 that will hopefully register with the European Community. And that blueprint or program will have to be clear on a number of points.

- It must spell out in unambiguous terms what West Africa and indeed the rest of Africa expects from Europe as a result of 1992. And high on that list of expectations is the need for increased official development aid (ODA), especially for the least developed of our countries, and it should aim to stimulate development. We also expect equal trade, increased direct investment, and the stabilization of commodity prices.

- That is what we expect of Europe. What does Europe in turn expect of us beyond the creation of a hospitable environment for investment by such measures as guarantees on the security of investments, a favorable tax regime, and the ability to repatriate a reasonable proportion of accrued profits? We do need to know and we hope to learn from our European colleagues.
- Let us have no illusions. If Africa is to have a fair deal in these coming changes, it will need to have in place the necessary leverage, or what American political scientists economy used to call countervailing power. Do we have such countervailing power? If not, how do we go about acquiring it?

We should not be disingenuous. The bald fact is that at present Africa does not have the leverage to treat on terms of equality with its European and other trading partners. But we do have the constituent elements with which to forge that leverage.

Will we now under the pressure of developments from outside be spurred into accelerating our efforts at regional and ultimately continental economic integration? If we do not in our turn achieve meaningful economic integration, it is unrealistic to hope in our disunity to secure a square deal from our trading partners.

2

SETTING THE PERSPECTIVE

Maria de Lourdes Pintasilgo

former Prime Minister of Portugal and Member of the European Parliament

From my vantage point as a member of the European Parliament and my political perception of what is going on in terms of this famous '92, I could develop its very positive aspects and fantastic effects on EEC itself and on Third World economics. It could be a new chance for exports from Third World countries, for diversification of their trade. A stronger EEC with an increased capacity could well increase development aid. Indeed, many of us are working toward that goal. This can already be seen with a certain similarity with what has happened with the weaker regions within the EEC itself—regions such as my own country Portugal, or Greece or Ireland or regions in decline such as Liverpool in England.

We could also say that a more unified EEC with common policies at all levels would be easier to deal with and would be a more direct and open partner. There would be more coherence and consistency in the different public policies. We are still very much in the beginning of truly common policies. We are just attempting to have common policies and we are dealing with different products one by one.

Instead, let me stress a few political points. In my own country, I tell my compatriots that '92 is not a mythical, remote date. '92 is already happening. Thanks to the cooperation between the European Commission and the European Parliament, and the final decisions of the European Council and the Council of Ministers, '92 is step by step already on its way. Most of the preparatory technical work has been done by the Commission, has been studied by the Parliament, and more than half of the directives needed have already been presented to the Council and to the governments of the member states. But in spite of these facts, some governments and even national parliaments do not seem to be noticing what is happening. In fact, it is in industry that the experts are more alert and more aware of the changes underway. With a monetary union, we would have more than 80 percent of the economic and monetary legislation of the member states issued at the community level. Such a fact will have enormous consequences for our partners.

First, their attention needs to be focused on those new events and about the free circulation of products. This requires that the members mobilize resources in terms of civil servants and experts and scrutinize what is happening and what is essential for their own economic planning.

Second, it is likely that a shift will occur in relation to some products within the EEC. Where will be the strength of the textile industry; where will be the new materials many people are interested in? EEC partners need to know more clearly who is selling and buying what, so that traditional practices, some inherited from the colonial past or the immediate postcolonial period, could be reviewed and adapted. For many of the European actors, the single market seems to be the only goal of the Single European Act. It is very important to stress that there will be a danger of a liberal market with a very high degree of competition, leaving no room for the weaker economy. Recently I visited compatriots who have been working in other EEC countries since 1961, when Angola and Mozambique started their liberation and many Portuguese people went to other parts of Europe. A group of them—simple people, manual workers—living in the Federal Republic of Germany asked: what is our country going to produce? Is it going to produce just the auxiliary things and services that we ourselves as workers have been doing in these brilliant and strong economies in the north of Europe? If we are not attentive, Portugal will be a region made up of well-treated, well-fed servants of rich families. Nobody wants that. I stress this extreme to say that this possibility also has a bearing on our partners as well. They could become providers of whatever commodities or labor the EEC may need. This is not because of any design of exploitation, but because of the sheer consequences of the liberal market. Many people in the parliament are concerned that we don't have a good scientific analysis of the eventual negative consequences of the single market. We need to have that picture in order to know how to cope with negative consequences and to take advantage of the positive ones so as to strengthen our own position.

We have to achieve the commitment goals of the single act:

- We have to draw the lines of what we call the European social space: social protection will be gradually harmonized, dialogue among the social partners will be fostered, and less prosperous regions will be specially cared for.
- We have to put into practice the multiannual program of R&D involving specially designed programs in different fields.
- We have to move quickly toward the monetary integration through a common currency and a federal bank.
- We have to attach a high priority to the environmental protection of the continent.

The importance of these goals is not only for Europe itself. They are very important for our partners who should also seek a parallel way in which all those goals should be realized. If Europe is able to give to social issues the same urgency it gives to the building up of a market, there are many more possibilities for a greater equality of opportunities between EEC and Third World countries. Social issues must be dealt with not as corrective but as an integral element of the entire process. There is an intimate correlation between what happens within the EEC countries and the relations between the EEC and the Southern Hemisphere. We are not only facing serious difficulties in harmonizing social issues, we are also facing a shortage of ideas, of new blood.

In most democracies we observe a major political shift. There is a very intimate kind of relationship, not to say dependency, between the prime minister and the minister of finance, and between the minister of finance and the governor of the central bank. When all decisions in Europe will be taken at the Community level, some reshuffling in political terms will be needed in the European countries. Africans should look at it and somehow also foresee the consequences.

A lot can be said about the question of the environment, for which alertness and a vigilant attitude are indispensable. The institutional bridge between the EEC and the south in this area, which currently constitutes the only predictable part of our relations, is the Lomé Conventions. These can be seen as a model for the relationship of the EEC with other regions. They do not represent just a generous attitude on the part of the EEC. The ACP countries are also a captive market for the EEC. This affords the ACP countries the possibility to exercise reverse pressures.

Lomé IV is not only an economic outlet. The ACP countries must also be seen from the point of view of the EEC as kind of political allies or political clients. Without political unity among the EEC, the ACP states are literally invaded by competing forces. In Angola, for instance, there is a division of labor that takes place among EEC member states present there. It is difficult for the people of Angola to see what is the policy of the EEC. But whenever the EEC moves toward more political unity, there will be a positive element for the ACP if we are on the same side of global or other issues. Lomé IV is also seen by the EEC, by all of us as the fulfillment of a sense of duty.

Personally, there are still two elements in Lomé IV that are quite different from the bilateral agreements and that can play a very important role in the future. One is the support given to the cooperative movements, small enterprises, and the establishment of nongovernmental organizations. This can be one way to involve fully the population in the development process and we can be sure that goals will be established jointly by all social forces. Another point is the role of women in development. This is not a projection of the European outlook. The role women play in West Africa in economy and in trade, is impressive, having an invisible and in many instances even visible role in leadership. I think this is very important for the future of West Africa.

Finally, let me outline what I see from our experience in building the Community in Europe as important for West Africa building its own community. First, we go beyond the nation state, and we will have the whole discussion of what is sovereignty. This is a fundamental question. Second, without the preparation of leadership at all levels, there is no end in what we are doing. Third, we need to rethink development in new terms: we are still using too much of the concepts of development from the 1950s and 1960s. We need to get away from too idealized concepts of development. One of the most important concerns in Europe was to build up the Europe of citizens, not just a connection among the leadership at the top. The EEC is not an intergovernmental organization. This means that we need to build a new type of relationship among people. Maybe if West Africa builds its own reality quickly enough, the ties existing in Africa beyond national boundaries will also become a source of inspiration for Europe, and we will learn from it.

Martin Bangemann
Vice President, European Commission

I want to deal with the possibilities and dangers stemming from the new development in Europe with regard to our political and, especially, economic relations.

What are we doing here? We are doing exactly what some regions in the world are doing as well, namely, developing regional cooperation. Regional cooperation is a new development throughout the world. It is true that the EEC has reached a very high degree of cohesiveness. If you compare the existence now of the EEC and the degree to which the economies of its 12 member states have grown closer to each other, it becomes obvious that this is perhaps the most promising type of regional cooperation; in comparison, for instance, to what the United States intends with Canada, a free trade zone; in comparison to some Arab countries, the Gulf Cooperation Council, for instance; in comparison with the ASEAN and some other even looser forms of cooperation in Africa and Latin America. It is quite clear that the EEC, for the time being, is the most advanced and consistent example of an integration process. The internal market is a further important step. It is true that the 12 markets of the 12 member states have already reached a certain degree of close cooperation, but there were and are obstacles to be a one and unique market of at least 320 million consumers with a high potential of purchasing power. This is what we are trying to do.

It is quite sure now that we will accomplish in 1992 that one single market, without technical barriers, without the taxation barriers that would impede a free trade exchange, and also without the physical border controls that are the obvious sign of national sovereignty. That in itself will give more growth and more economic power to the Community. We estimate that about 3.7– 3.8 percent of economic growth that we reached in the last two years are due one-third to the idea of the common internal market. The prospect of it has evidently made the community more attractive both for internal investment and for external investment. We have a lot of investment from other countries inside that market. Of course, that means more growth, more jobs, and more economic possibilities. That by itself is not a danger for our trading partners, especially not a danger for our partners in Africa because economic growth always means more imports and more economic chances. So it should not be in the first instance negative.

Of course, despite all the benefits, the internal market is not only a source of euphoria but also a source of some concern. We do understand those concerns, and it is for that reason that I wish to discuss the possibilities and also the dangers. We should in future combine all the efforts that will be continued in the framework of the Lomé Convention with some new means of introducing economic cooperation, for instance, by private investment. The fears that may be there are also the fears of industrialized countries if they are looking at the European Community's economic strength. Their fear is certainly not unfounded since the internal market should and will strengthen the overall competitiveness of the Community. One of the aims of the internal market is to strengthen the competitiveness of European industry. But all experience shows that in case there is a certain solidarity, as exists between Europe and the ACP countries, higher competitiveness also gives more means for economic cooperation. Take, for example, Portugal. When Portugal and Spain were about to enter the Community, there was widespread discussion in both countries whether they could stand the competition of such highly efficient countries as Great Britain, France, or the Federal Republic of Germany. The reality now is that since they entered, the gross rate of both countries is the highest of all countries in Europe. Why? Since they are an element of the European market, investment is going to Portugal and Spain. It is quite true that investment looks for a good place. A good place for investment is a place that is in a market or has established links with a market into which you want to produce and that has low production costs. It is true that the possibilities of Portugal and Spain in comparison with the countries named above are a little less advantageous; at the same time this has been to their advantage to get more investment than anybody else. The textile industry of Portugal, for instance, is an example of a growing industry. The automobile industry in Spain is causing fear to the industry in Germany because Spain is producing the same effective cars at much lower costs.

This shows that it is not true that in itself a country with less possibilities than others is lost in a competition, provided that this country is taking advantage of investment (both public and private) and provided that the climate for investment is good there. Then you have an immediate advantage that is not to be planned, maybe cannot be planned or only to a certain extent, that is stemming from private investment and the competitiveness from the liberal market system.

I am a liberal. I have always lived with the conviction that a market system is more effective and by being more effective is socially more just than any other system. I am not convinced by the idea but by the effectiveness and by the results we have had. Germany was completely destroyed after World War II; it was politically isolated. We started again and the moment we had the market system available, there was the so-called German economic wonder, and we have been making our way on behalf of that system. Now look at the East European states. They are abandoning their system because they know it has no effect. It is not a question of ideological positions, it is a question of effectiveness. History is different. The political background of many African countries will not and cannot be the same as European countries. But African countries should do what East European countries are trying to do. At least, combine elements of the market system, private investment, with their systems at home to make the system more effective and by that getting new chances in the European internal market. We should discuss this also in the framework of the Lomé Convention.

The concerns that have been expressed by developing countries are, of course, to a certain extent justified, because the systems we have had up to now—both the European system and the bilateral national systems—more or less depend on preference systems. That is to say, they are based on trade, on trade advantages. Both the internal market and the ongoing Uruguay round are meant to abolish the obstacles to free trade. Even if we can get to 100 percent, it is quite clear that the intent is to get away from these barriers to free trade, customs, etc. We are realizing that the advantage systems will have no advantage at all. Because if there is a zero level of duties or customs, you cannot get an advantage by having a zero level because it is available for everybody. It is true that the developing countries' fears are not wholly unfounded. Competition will get tougher throughout the world and we will reach more freedom of trade and by that the dismantling of what are now known as the preferential systems. If that is so, the completion of the internal market also requires the abolition of national quantitative restrictions. That in itself is something of a new possibility to most of our trading partners. There will be no replacement of national quantitative restrictions by European quantitative restrictions. That, of course, is very important for developing countries because normally we have quantitative restrictions less for developing countries than for the newly industrialized nations. That in itself is a danger for the import of these products. The main import restrictions for the developing countries are in the textiles sector. The Community has declared itself willing to return to the general GATT rules in the international textiles trade as soon as possible. This also diminishes the importance of special preferences for developing countries; it is opening up quite a new possibility—not only in the trade with the EEC. When we started that discussion in the Uruguay round, the traditional countries for textile production, such as India and Pakistan, were very much asking for getting away with the restrictions of the MFA (Multi Fibre Agreement). When we are doing away with these restrictions, we said that this cannot only mean that India and Pakistan are free to import their textiles into Europe; it also means that other developing countries must be free to export to India and Pakistan and to the newly industrialized countries such as Singapore, Hong Kong, Taiwan, and Korea. When they realized that, the interest was a little less active. That shows that there are ample opportunities for everybody, especially those nations that regard themselves as weakest. Weakness in itself is not only a disadvantage, it is a chance if you get into closer cooperation with a stronger partner. Europe is able and willing to give that cooperation.

What shall we do and what is to be done? The strong Community in itself is useful for the developing countries and our partners in the ACP agreements. The internal market will strengthen the Community both economically and politically and this, of course, is to the benefit of West Africa in our arrangement of cooperation. The consistency of development policies in the long term is strengthened by the integration of the Community, and it leads also to greater effectiveness. The influence of the Community in national bodies will increase, and therefore West Africa should not have fear that Europe is becoming strong. If we wanted to become a fortress, then, of course, that fear would be justified. But we are not willing to be a fortress and we are not about to be a fortress. We want to continue our open and cooperative position, and therefore our strength will be a strength for others as well.

Of course, we will have to do something in addition. Let us discuss new possibilities of economic cooperation. For instance, if you look at the regional cooperation and the readiness of the different regional entities to cooperate with each other, you will see that there is that ample possibility in the EEC with a readiness to enlarge that. We have already had discussions with EFTA countries—the six Western democracies that are not members of the EEC. We also have concluded an agreement with COMECON and bilateral agreements with the member states of COMECON. We have a new arrangement with the Gulf Cooperation Council. We have a longer dating arrangement with ASEAN; China is most interested to get into a closer relationship with Europe. This shows a stretch of a part of the world that is about to cooperate more closely. If you look at the Pacific Basin you will find that the United States and Canada, together with Japan and other countries, such as, Australia and New Zealand, are trying to bring about something for the Pacific rim. In Latin America there are slight chances of regional cooperation and also in Africa, of course. But is there a sufficient link between Africa and that great region of Europe—EEC, EFTA, Eastern Europe—Arab countries, ASEAN, and China? This is the question. Have we already reached a sufficient level of political and economic cooperation between Europe and Africa? My answer is no. This is the problem.

In the future, the traditional framework of development policy will not be the real basis for economic cooperation. It will be the cooperation between the private economies and private firms, which is lacking between Africa and Europe. We should therefore discuss if the environment in Africa is ready enough for investment. Have we to work on the legal conditions whatever they are? Are we in Europe prepared enough to have a practical framework? Is there, for instance, a guarantee if investments are carried out in Africa—insurance etc.? Is there a framework from the side of Europe to foster and to back private investment? Can we discuss and define in which regions private investment would be useful? Is it possible that some member states of the Lomé Convention would be more ready than others to accept private investment in showing others who are more reluctant what the effects are? I do not believe in the discussion that we will then have the great international influence of multinationals and all that. That is fine if somebody politically does not want foreign investment, it is up to him. Nobody will impose on you these possibilities. If you say no, we don't want them because we consider Fiat, Unilever, Mercedes Benz, or whatever it is, as a multinational firm which is trying to bring a political power into our country, it is up to you. It is fine, we are not pressing anybody. But if somebody is ready to cooperate in that way, also with small and medium-size enterprises, also in the qualification of the workers, which is one of the basic elements of the social dimension of the European Community which was discussed here. Social dimension does not mean that we want to pay helpless people. We want to qualify helpless people. Qualify them so that they can participate in that competition. This is possible. This is most effectively done by private investment because normally private enterprises are much more interested in having qualified people than anything else because that is the basis of their competitiveness. We are doing that also with East European countries. We have joint ventures. We are discussing tax agreements to avoid double taxation. There are agreements on ensuring the security of capital investment. There are agreements on intellectual property etc. This is the whole legal framework and if somebody among you is ready to enter with us into such a discussion I promise you that in a couple of years you will have much more development, together with the integration of the internal market in Europe than with decades of the old policy, that does not have the effect of bringing you into that regional cooperation world in which we are living now. We are happy, Europeans are happy to have that possibility. But I do believe that it is necessary to work on a common possibility with you. That is my message. It is a very clear pragmatic message. It is an offer. Everybody is free to say yes or no. I hope that most of you will say yes and that we can meet again in five years time and then you could say that 1992 was a very happy event. Some years ago, in '92 America was discovered; now in 1992 Europe is to be discovered.

Questions and Answers

Olusegun Obasanjo. If 1992 will be the year that Europe will be discovered, maybe you can tell us the year Africa will be rediscovered. You speak of creating a hospitable environment for foreign investment and do not go beyond that. When one talks of creating a hospitable environment for foreign investment, one is talking of creating a hospitable environment for local investment and for foreign investment, because part of the hospitable environment you have to create for foreign investment is the interest of the local investors. If local people are not investing, you will wonder what is happening here. But what they do say is that we have gone the whole length of all the things required—structural adjustment, providing a very good tax regime, even some guaranteeing foreign investment. Some have even put it into their constitution that under no circumstances will foreign investment be expropriated. In spite of this, we do not seem to be getting as much as we would like to have. What more do you want us to do? What are really the ingredients of creating a hospitable environment for foreign investment for Europe?

Bangemann. If the legal framework is already in place, I cannot ask for more. A guarantee for investment is, of course, not a guarantee for good results and profits of investment. It is just a legal basis for investment. To avoid double taxation is more or less a normal situation between countries that are mutually investing. So if that exists, that is fine. This is then, of course, the basis for the above question and the justification to ask what more shall we do. In that case I can only tell you that we are to do more. Because I do believe that, and we are doing much to foster investment in some East European countries—for instance, there is a guarantee system if you are exporting capital goods, even in some cases for services by some member states. That is a system that is partly paid by fees of those that are exporting, a sort of insurance system. Partly it is covered by public guarantees, so that if there is a loss of the insurance system the public budget pays. That is one of the lacking possibilities.

Second, we have ample possibilities of having investment capital from banks; not only from private banks but also from public banks. Certainly we have committees that are meeting not only on the political level but on the level of businessmen; given the possibilities of information, creating joint ventures for instance. Joint venture is a form in which local investors must be interested, because if you get a joint venture this is, of course, of mutual benefit—for the local investor because he gets a good investment and for the foreign investor because he gets a partner with a knowledge of the local market and of the local conditions. We should and we are about to work out a system in the EEC concerning how we can interest private capital investment to go more to Africa in order to reinforce these ties—as we did in the case of Portugal and Spain. Of course, there is a difference because Portugal and Spain, which are member states of the European Community. But, notwithstanding that difference, the moment when these possibilities were there, private capital came into these countries, and that is the source of their economic growth now.

Akin Mabogunje. What about the sort of developments that are taking place with the Uruguay round, etc? Do you foresee the demise of the preferential agreements, the Lomé Convention, the ACP Convention? What about aspects of the monetary union?

Bangemann. The Uruguay round is meant to end in two years' time. We attempted to have a midway review in Montreal at the end of 1988 and that failed. But we have reached a consensus now in Geneva so that it is not beyond any possibility that we can use the next two years to bring about a result. This result will be a clear cut of taxes and customs and duties and, for instance, in textiles, a getting back to the normal rules of the GATT system, maybe with a transitional period. If you look at textiles, the system of quotas, which was one of the possibilities of giving preferences, not only duties and customs, but also giving quotas, will be diminished in that vital sector of economic activities. The tendency is in general to remove or to reduce the traditional barriers to trade. If that is done, then preference systems lose their importance because if you have a zero level of customs, how can you give a preference to somebody? If you don't have quotas, how can you give double, triple, or complete freedom to somebody? That is the problem.

The monetary union is not an aim of the internal market. The aim in the framework of the internal market is more freedom for capital movements. We are about to do that. There are restrictions for capital movement in the European Community by some member states. You can't, for instance, freely transfer currencies from any member state into another one. But we are removing that, and member states are cooperating. So it is true and a real pragmatic aim that at the end of 1992 there will be no restrictions for the free movement of capital in the community. But we won't have in 1992 a monetary union, because it is not in the program. As noted in the quite recent report of the president of the Commission who presided a committee on the monetary union, that is an accepted goal. But nobody expects it to be reached in 1992; maybe by the year 2000 we can come to a European currency. I believe it will be step by step. We can develop the ECU into a parallel currency, but I don't think that before the year 2000 we will replace the national currencies.

As you know, we are harmonizing our technical standards. It would be of the utmost importance for the possibilities of exporting goods and services from West African countries into the internal market that there is early information on what we are doing in that field of harmonization of standards, and a possibility of cooperating with West African organizations that are dealing with the problem of standardization. To give a very concrete example, we have already left the phase of research and development and are beginning production of a high definition television. That is a major development in telecommunications. We are developing standards. The Japanese are developing standards as well. It is of mutual interest that Europe could go to African countries and that we could agree on European standards because that would reinforce the position of the European telecommunications industry. If West Africa has, for instance, the same standards, there is, of course, ample possibility for investment in some West African countries in order to produce elements for the industry in your countries, because then we belong to the same family of the same standards. These are very practical questions.

In Europe in the mid-1980s, to give another example, there was a certain form of so-called Eurosclerosis, there was a Euro-pessimism. A Southeast Asian prime minister remarked that Europe was a nice region of the world: "As a tourist I like Europe, but the economy, forget about it. You have no chance whatsoever against us." Now, they fear Europe. Things have totally changed. That is partly due to the fact that we have built up not only an idea that was already there, but the practical experience and the practical possibility. Even the discussion about the fortress Europe has had its positive side effect. We are not willing to build a fortress Europe. But since everybody believes that we are doing it, they come into Europe with their investments.

Pierre-Claver Damiba

Assistant Administrator and Director
Regional Bureau for Africa, UNDP

The main issues under discussion at the conference on West Africa are:

1. It is most important for the African countries to initiate their response to a united Europe early so as not to be overtaken by events. Meetings such as in Brussels can set into motion that process. We in Africa are so concerned with the day-to-day business and the short-term problems that sometimes it is difficult to look at the horizon. The integration of Europe is so important for us that the sooner we can start having a clear vision of it and drawing conclusions and consequences for our economic organization in West Africa, the better.

2. Fears in many quarters in Africa derive from the fact that
   (a) despite independence, the external economic policies of many African countries are still linked to the former metropolitan countries;
   (b) the African economies are in a difficult transitional stage with many of them battling with difficult structural reforms; which make new external factors somewhat unwelcome;
   (c) the economic management capacity of the countries is weak; many of them have not been able to exploit the existing opportunities of external trade and investment; and
   (d) African regional cooperation efforts have failed to achieve a substantive integration, which places the individual countries in a weak bargaining position.

3. There are advantages that may result from a united Europe for the African economies. These include an enlarged market for African products; the opening up of hitherto closed sections of Europe; the possibility of joint venture. European integration should have a demonstration effect in spurring Africans to take seriously their own integration.

4. Success for the African countries will depend on
   (a) the success of their own internal structural reforms to compete effectively with other LDCs who may have equal access to the Community;
   (b) concessions that could be gained through their principal allies (especially France in this case) in negotiating a revised treaty;
   (c) progress with Africa's own integration efforts;
   (d) the building of capacity through training; the United Nations Development Programme (UNDP) and the ECOWAS/ECA secretariat could play leading roles in capacity building; and

(c) their capacity to develop private sector, to create an enabling environment for both indigenous and foreign investors, for multinational companies as well as small- and medium-scale enterprises.

5. African countries will not be able to greatly influence the course of European integration. The process is in motion. What they can do is to exploit the opportunities that will open up for which the African nations would require equipment to meet the challenges of stiffer competition, and they can learn the rules of trading with a multilateral Europe. The old issue here is the extent to which African countries can transform their comparative advantages into actual competitive advantage in the world market.

6. Indeed, this matter is so important that the Africa Leadership Forum could be requested to establish and lead an *expert group* to explore more in detail the problem for sub-Saharan Africa as a whole. The conference here in Brussels, those already organized earlier in Franceville and Gabon, and others underway within the ECA provide a solid background for such studies. UNDP could provide some budgetary support if necessary with the hope that other funding agencies may join and support the exercise.

7. Through such joint and early endeavors, West African countries will be better prepared to take the challenge of European integration in order to pursue their own economic integration as the only valid response and alternative to the development process in sub-Saharan Africa. The region must be made more competitive in a world where the basic rule is not the state but the extent to which private enterprises and entities can compete and win and sustain growth to ensure that the easing of poverty will be better addressed.

Alhaji Abubaker Alhaji
Minister of Budget and Planning, Nigeria

The flow of investment to West African countries from industrialized nations depends as much on economic and monetary stability as on political stability in Africa. In Europe and other democracies, investors are not directed to go to country X or country Y. It depends on the individual corporate decision of a bank or a construction company or an enterprise within the community to decide whether country X provides an attractive investment climate and meets all its criteria for investment before it goes there. Nobody in Europe, not even in Brussels, can direct it to go there. So, in addition to having political stability, Africa must also have other social infrastructure, including security, to attract foreign investors. In essence what I am saying is that if we are going to or we want to live like the white man, we have to work hard like the white man. The decision to complete the process of integration of the European market by 1992 seems now irrevocable. Indeed, it may be desirable from the African point of view. There is no need for African nations to be apprehensive about this.

What we need is to think positively and to encourage constructive reactions as to how to turn this development to our advantage. I hope this will be our guiding principle. We should take steps now, hence the wisdom of the seminar, to ensure that decisions taken regarding external economic relations between the Community are not disadvantageous to us. The secretariat of the ACP in Brussels should perhaps be more alert. Every move of the Community, whether monetary, economic, or in other spheres, has been monitored by West African nations. We can start lobbying, so that by the time the decision is taken, at least our views on the subject will have been made known to those in a position to make the decision. We should also ensure that the existing concessions we have, on a bilateral basis, are not diminished and perhaps are replaced by the whole Community adopting them. We have, of course, some preferential treatment now. We need to ensure that those treatments that are given on a country-to-country basis will be accepted on a Community basis so that we have the advantage of a wider market than the individual countries with which we now have arrangements. West Africa relies to a great extent on the Community's market. It is our principal source of aid. We have cultural and educational links with Europe, particularly with respect to West Africa. So we start with the advantage that we should exploit rather than be pessimistic about or surrender to it.

There are some areas of particular concern in the process of the Community's integration, the area of immigration, for instance, and export credit policies. Access to Western institutions will enable us to develop the technology with which we can eventually be self-reliant or competitive. But at the moment we must learn the technology, and unless we have access to Western institutions—the universities, polytechnics, etc.—we will not be in a position to come anywhere near being competitive. The export credit policy is very important to us. We may have abundant natural resources, but unless we have the capital to develop those resources they will remain where the are, where they have been for the last few millions of years. At the moment there is an embryo organization that is in the Paris Club where we meet all these OECD country members and discuss rescheduling or availability of new money for our countries on a case-by-case basis. I can foresee a situation where, after 1992, we are faced with one common interest rate for all the member countries of the EEC. We should start working hard now to ensure that interest is one of the areas that warrants subsidy, because the role of interest rates has not been sufficiently recognized in international trade. It is very important. For Nigeria, the rise in interest rate and the decision taken by the United States cost us in 1989 alone about $400 million extra. These are little things that have been crippling our economy and increasing our debt burden. We do not seem to care about them. This seminar should recommend that a monetary and economic monitoring unit be set up, and if one exists now, it should be strengthened in the ACP secretariat for monitoring developments in the EEC toward integration, so that we will be in a position to follow them up and make sure that they are decided in a way that will minimize their adverse effects on our economies.

3

COMPLETING THE EUROPEAN MARKET

Carol Lancaster
Professor, Georgetown University, Washington, DC

Introduction

I address myself to two areas here. One is the likely impact of Europe 1992 on West Africa, and the second concerns how it is that the EEC has been relatively successful and ECOWAS relatively unsuccessful in their integration experiments. What is the difference between these two experiments, and what if anything can be done to impart of impel greater success in the ECOWAS effort to create an economic union among its 16 member countries?

First, Europe 1992 is an exercise in deregulation, an exercise in removal of nontariff barriers to trade among Europeans. It is not an exercise in monetary union, although that very removal of the nontariff barriers may propel the Europeans further toward monetary union. It is not an exercise in reforming the cultural policy, which would be of considerable interest in West Africa. I am not as relaxed as some others about some of the potential implications of removing the nontariff barriers to intra-European trade, mainly I think because we don't know in many cases what is going to replace them. There are a number of nontariff barriers now: technical standards, health standards, fiscal policies that differ from country to country, immigration policies, border controls, and individual bilateral trading arrangements between European and non-EEC countries. These are going to be changed if the Europeans succeed in achieving their goals in 1992. From my side of the Atlantic, there is some skepticism that this will be achieved. Maybe that is wishful thinking on the part of my countrymen. But there is some skepticism about some of these goals. Nevertheless, assuming they will be achieved, we still don't know what will be put in place of the nontariff barriers. Take the case of bananas. There are individual protocols between individual European countries and banana-producing countries of West Africa and Central America. If I am not mistaken the Germans import bananas from Central America at a somewhat lower price than France imports bananas from the Ivory Coast. These arrangements are going to be changed, but I don't think it is clear yet what is going to be put in their place and which countries will benefit and which countries will not. Will the bananas now come from Central America for the entire EEC? Or, how will the Ivory Coast and other African banana exporters fit into the new regime? I only raise this one among many as a possible thing to watch.

Again, in Washington, there has been quite of bit of concern about the implementation of the European-wide health standard on beef imports. My countrymen may be overexercised about this one, but it has been seen there as a sign that what will be put in place, in some cases at least, is stricter Community-wide standards on what is imported, and that contributes to this fear of Europe becoming a fortress as nontariff barriers are removed and something is put in its place around the entire Community. Again, it seems that these are not things to become apprehensive about, but I agree that these kind of changes need monitoring for countries that are concerned and are likely to be affected by them. More than just monitoring but actually to stay ahead of what is being considered and to impart one's views before decisions are made is a very important thing to bear in mind. Once decisions are made, it is very hard to unmake them.

The impact of Europe 1992, if it succeeds, is likely to stimulate growth in the Community, although there are several different estimates of how much growth is stimulated. But even the least optimistic estimates do see growth being stimulated. This in some sense ought to be of benefit to West Africa. West African countries are mainly exporters of primary products and normally, when there is not surplus production, economic growth will stimulate the demand for primary products. Hopefully this growth, which is likely to take place in the Community, will spill over with benefits to West Africa. There are other aspects of this, however. Eventually, West Africa will probably want to produce and export manufactured goods to the Community. The questions then become: what are going to be the conditions of entry, and are they going to be any more difficult in five or 10 years than they are today? They might be more difficult simply because the Community is likely to become more competitive and that will make it necessary for African manufactured good exports to become more competitive to get into the Community.

The other question, of course, comes back to what kind of rules and regulations are going to replace the nontariff barriers that are going to be eliminated. Will those rules and regulations have an impact on manufactured goods exports to the Community? The literature I have seen from parts of the developing world where countries are exporting manufactured goods is now reflecting a concern about access to the Community. Again, well based or not, it is a concern for the newly industrializing countries, and so on. On the question of why the Community is more successful in its efforts at achieving economic integration and ECOWAS is really quite disappointing at achieving any progress on economic integration, I have suggested two major differences that I think are important. One is the economic differences between the Community and West African members of ECOWAS. When the Community was set up, there was some prospect of mutual benefit in the expanded trade that was expected to take place mainly between Germany and France—manufactured goods exports for agricultural exports. It seems that in West Africa and other parts of the developing world with economies that are complementary or supplementary, the opportunities for exchange are much more limited. So, removal of tariff barriers can bring costs immediately. Some of these have already been mentioned—reduction in government revenues, etc. But the benefits, which ultimately are mainly in the form of new investment in these areas, are going to be over the long term and sometimes very indefinite, which creates an economic problem of costs being immediate and benefits being long-term. At least it does not surprise me that African leaders sign on to these agreements, agree to reduce tariff barriers and move toward integration, but then don't implement those agreements because there are very few politicians who are willing to take costs now for benefits 5, 10, 15 years down the road. That is a major problem here.

The other problem in the economic area is that when there are benefits they tend to be concentrated in one or two countries. The East African common market fell apart very much because Kenya was enjoying the benefits of increased investment and there was really no way that the Kenyans were willing or able to compensate the Tanzanians for what the Tanzanians considered as lost investment opportunities. So that becomes another problem of the efforts at economic integration among developing countries. The compensation of losers.

One other cluster of issues that seems important is that the European Community has come together under some external pressure—the pressure of a uncertain political situation on the eastern border. Direct pressure from the

United States at the very beginning of the effort at integration, etc. ECOWAS was created very much as a result of Nigerian diplomacy. The Nigerians then lost interest in ECOWAS, or at least were not pushing it so hard, no more pressures on neighbors to join. At the same time there was a good deal of skepticism among some Francophone countries as to whether they really wanted to get into an economic union with Nigeria; the literature suggests a good deal of skepticism on the part of the French as well. So, in a sense the ECOWAS experiment has had pressures on it running in the opposite direction of the European pressures.

What can be done? It does seem that there is an opportunity for the EEC, now increasingly successful in its experiment in integration, to help ECOWAS revitalize its own experiment in integration. One of a number of possibilities might simply be to jointly identify an area or sector in the ECOWAS region in which integration might be easily promoted. The Europeans could provide some financing or guarantees or stimulate investment. Perhaps some compensatory financing for countries that would not benefit, something to get the integration experiment moving in West Africa. The EEC has done something very similar with the Central American common market; can it do less for West Africa with which the EEC has had such long and close relationships?

Implications for West Africa

In 1987 the European Economic Community (EC) unanimously ratified the Single European Act, committing its member states to complete the integration of the European market by the end of 1992. Achievement of the goals of the act is expected to reduce the costs of production and trade and so boost economic growth and employment in the EC; promote research and development of a size and sophistication that would allow the Community to compete with the United States and Japan in technologically advanced markets; and enhance the strength and bargaining power of the EC on international economic issues.

It is not clear at present what the economic impact of completing the EC market will be on the rest of the world, including the 16 countries of West Africa. (Benin, Cape Verde, the Cote d'Ivoire, Burkina Faso, the Gambia,

Ghana, Guinea, Guinea-Bissau, Liberia, Mali, Mauritania, Niger, Nigeria, Senegal, Sierra Leone, and Togo). Much will depend on what kind of Community-wide policies governing external economic relations are adopted as the remaining barriers to the free movement of goods, services, capital, and labor among Community members are removed. These changes could provide encouragement for renewed efforts at economic integration by the Economic Community of West African States (ECOWAS). The EC has long served as a model for economic integration in ECOWAS and elsewhere in Africa as well as in other developing regions. The success of the EC in furthering its own integration can provide reassurance to those struggling to promote integration in West Africa that their goals are achievable. The EC's experience can also offer lessons and insights for Africans on how they might overcome the obstacles to their own integration efforts. The EC itself may be able to offer direct support for progress toward economic union in West Africa.

This chapter explores each of these issues: the meaning and consequences of completing the EC market; the possible impact of completing the EC market on West Africa; and the lessons of European integration for the Economic Community of West African States.

Completing the EC Market: Meaning and Consequences

The European Economic Community now includes 12 countries and a total population of 320 million. Member countries already have common external tariffs and have eliminated internal tariffs. They also have a common agricultural policy, which attempts to ensure Community-wide prices and markets for agricultural goods. However, nontariff barriers to trade in goods and services, and controls on the movement of people and capital have persisted.

To complete the EC market, nontariff barriers and other impediments to the free movement of goods, services, labor, and capital must be removed or harmonized. Such barriers include varying technical specifications and standards for traded commodities, different qualifications for individuals providing professional services, differing tax regimes, and physical controls at borders to govern the movement of people and goods. Special trading arrangements between Community members and foreign countries, including arrangements governing imports of bananas, textiles, footwear, and nearly 1,000 other goods and services must also be eliminated. In most cases, individual country arrangements will be replaced by EC-wide arrangements of some kind. Completing the EC market does not involve changes in the common agricultural policy, nor at this point, the establishment of a monetary union among EC member states.

Progress thus far toward achieving the goals of the Single European Act includes ratification of the act itself and the adoption of roughly 100 out of the 300 regulations necessary to completing the EC market. Decision making on these regulations is based on qualified majority voting, an important change from the system of unanimous voting used in EC decision making in the past. The most contentious regulations have yet to be passed. These include elimination of border controls, harmonization of taxation, and external trade policies.

Completing the EC market is intended to produce the following consequences:

- To lower the costs of production for EC industrial firms by providing the economies of scale associated with larger markets and by reducing the costs of trading associated with physical and bureaucratic barriers to trade, such as internal customs clearances at borders.
- To lower the prices of goods and services traded by encouraging greater competition among producers of similar goods throughout the EC.
- To promote research and development in high technology, large-scale production lines, which can only occur efficiently in large markets.
- As a result of these benefits, to increase investment, employment, and growth in the EC. According to the EC Commission, removing nontariff barriers within the EC could produce as much as a 7 percent increase in Gross Domestic Product, five million new jobs, and a 4.5 percent decrease in consumer prices over the medium term.

There are three major uncertainties associated with EC efforts to complete its market. First, will the EC in fact be able to agree on the difficult changes required to complete the market? There are already concerns on the part of some countries, for example, the UK, about the security implications of eliminating frontier controls. Member governments, e.g., France, have shown some wariness about harmonizing taxes if such harmonization would lead to a decrease in government revenues.

Second, what will be the economic impact of removal of nontariff barriers? One immediate impact may be a shift in the demand for goods and services from higher cost, less competitive national producers to lower cost producers in other EC countries. If higher cost producers are unable to increase their productivity and compete, they will be forced out of business. It is possible that completing the market could have a depressing effect on employment and economic activity in particular regions or sectors in the short run. This, in turn, could lead to a drop in the demand for imports (including goods imported from West Africa) in those regions. However, there is no expectation that adverse economic consequences of this type will be widespread or long in duration. There is little dispute that the long-run impact of these changes will be to stimulate economic growth, although there are disagreements about how much additional growth will result.

Third, what will be the impact of completing the market on the rules and regulations governing the Community's external trade? This is the issue of greatest concern to the rest of the world. Foreign governments fear that internal nontariff barriers and single-country trade arrangements will be replaced with higher nontariff barriers to imports from outside the EC. Community officials have argued that fears of a "fortress Europe" are unjustified. It is still too early to be sure whether these fears are warranted or groundless.

The Impact of Europe 1992 on West Africa

Before speculating on the impact of completion of the EC market on West Africa, it is worth reviewing existing economic links between the 16 countries of West Africa and the EC.

Trade relations between the EC and the West African 16 show the following characteristics:

- The EC remains the major trading partner of most of the West Africa 16, amounting to over half of the total exports of many of those countries.
- At the same time, the total value of West African trade with the EC has fallen over the past several years as the volume of West African exports has stagnated or fallen and as prices for commodities exported by West African countries have dropped.
- Reliance on the EC as an export market has diminished over the last decade for almost all countries of West Africa (with Nigeria as the major exception).
- The vast majority of the exports of the West African 16 to Europe are primary products, including cotton, coffee, cocoa, iron, ore, timber, fish, fruits and vegetables, phosphate, and petroleum.

Up-to-date statistics on private direct and portfolio investment by the EC 12 in the West African 16 are not available, but several things are clear from current statistics on overall investment in these countries as well as from past data on private flows by source. First, for most of West Africa, private direct and portfolio investment has been stagnant or falling during much of the 1980s. The only country that shows a rising trend in private flows is Guinea, where changes in policies encouraging private investment have stimulated investor interest. Second, much of the private investment in West Africa has come from the EC, with France, the UK, and Germany as the principal sources. This is likely still to be the case, although Japanese investment in Africa has been growing. The United States remains a minor investor throughout much of sub-Saharan Africa, with some concentration of direct investments in Liberia and Nigeria.

Regarding concessional aid, the EC, including the European Development Fund (EDF) and aid from individual EC member states, was the largest single source of foreign aid for all but two of the West African 16 in 1987. Aid from EC members and the EDF exceeded 40 percent of total net concessional aid disbursements in 11 West African countries, and for nine of these countries, that percentage rose between 1984 and 1987.

Statistics cannot capture fully the extent of economic links between West Africa and the EC. All West African countries, plus 50 other African, Caribbean, and Pacific (ACP) countries are part of the Lome Agreement with the EC, which provides preferential access to the EC market for certain exports from developing country members of the agreement and for financial and technical cooperation among ACP countries and the EC. Negotiations are just getting underway on the fourth Lome Agreement.

Finally, seven West African countries—Benin, Burkina Faso, the Cote d'Ivoire, Mali, Niger, Senegal, and Togo—are members of the Union Monetaire Ouest Africaine (UMOA), one of only three monetary unions that exist today among independent countries. (The other two are the monetary union among five central African countries and France and the Rand area between Lesotho, Swaziland, and the Republic of South Africa.) With a common currency tied to the French franc, these countries enjoy particularly close monetary and financial links with that country.

To sum up, economic links between the West African 16 and the EC 12 remain close. The EC remains West Africa's major export market and principal source of aid, although in the area of trade, West African reliance on the EC market is gradually declining. How is completion of the European market likely to affect these relations?

In the short run, the elimination of internal, nontariff barriers to trade in goods and services within the EC may not have any significant impact on West Africa. Most West African exports to the EC are primary products not directly affected by the changes in nontariff barriers. (They are likely to be more affected by any agreements emerging from the Uruguay Round of GATT tariff negotiations, which may reduce the margin of preference enjoyed by West African countries to the EC under the Lome Agreement.) However, there are a number of areas where changes, as yet uncertain, associated with completing the EC market could affect West African interests and should remain a legitimate sourc of concern to these countries until those changes are clarified.

First, what EC-wide arrangements will replace current bilateral arrangements governing imports of bananas, textiles, footwear, and other products that West African countries now export or might be able to export to the EC in the near future? Will EC-wide arrangements be more or less restrictive than those currently faced by West African exporters?

Second, what EC-wide arrangements will be put in place to govern health standards and technical specifications governing imports from abroad? Will they be more or less restrictive than those facing West Africans today? Concerns about standards governing beef and phosphates imports have already been raised.

Third, how will harmonization of taxes within the EC affect the price and demand for imports from West Africa? Where tax harmonization results in an overall increase in the taxes on goods imported from West Africa or on goods using imported inputs from West Africa (e.g., chocolate candy), demand for these imports may fall. Similarly, a decrease in the taxes on West African exports to the EC or on goods using them as inputs could produce an increase in demand for those goods.

Fourth, how will EC policies on immigration affect West Africans? Will Europe '92 have more restrictive immigration regulations than exist at present in individual countries?

Fifth, what changes will EC member countries make in their export credit programs as they approach completion of their market? There are already reports on the need to unify export credit policies and the possibility of creating a EC-wide export credit agency. How will any of these changes affect access by West African countries to export credits from the EC?

Sixth, if the short-run economic impact of completing the EC market is recessionary, how will that affect the EC demand for primary product imports from West Africa?

The long-run impact on West Africa of completing the EC market is likely to be more significant than the short-run impact. But whether it will be positive or negative is equally unclear. If economic growth accelerates in the EC, that growth could be translated into increased demand for West African exports, particularly of minerals and agricultural raw materials used in industrial production.

In the long run West African countries will want to become producers and exporters of manufactured goods. The EC market will remain an important one for them. If new regulations (involving trade, health, or technical specifications) governing imports of textiles and other light manufactures prove to be more restrictive than those currently in place, that market may be even more difficult to penetrate than at present, possibly discouraging investment in manufacturing for export from West Africa to the EC.

The changes leading to "Europe 1992" may also have implications for the flow of investment to West Africa. If completing the EC market stimulates increased investment in Europe (either by EC or by foreign firms), there may be a smaller flow of investment to West Africa.

Removal of nontariff barriers within the EC could well put further pressures on member states to move toward monetary union. It will be difficult, for example, to operate monetary compensation arrangements on intra-EC trade in agricultural goods. Such arrangements now rely on border controls for implementation. Indeed, each step toward economic integration tends to increase pressures for yet further steps. If there should be a move toward monetary union among EC states, the question of how to handle the Union Monetaire Ouest Africaine will inevitably arise. It is generally recognized that the CFA franc is currently overvalued, encouraging imports and probably costing CFA countries export markets at a time when most of them need to increase exports and reduce imports. The overevaluation of the CFA and the weakness of the banking and financial systems generally in CFA countries also represent a cost, actual and potential, to the French treasury. Would a combination of financial problems in the UMOA plus a move toward monetary union in the EC force a reorganization or possibly even the elimination of the CFA area? These questions are already being quietly raised in West Africa and even in the World Bank and IMF. And what would the economic effects of a dissolution of the CFA area be on its West African members as well as West African countries that are not members? Would it spur economic integration among ECOWAS countries by dissolving a possible barrier to integration, the separate monetary union among a group of ECOWAS member states—about which countries not members of the franc zone have long been concerned. The economic changes wrought by a completion of the European market by 1992 promise to be of major importance, both for Europeans and much of the rest of the world. Because many details of the changes needed to achieve the goals of the Single European Act are unclear, West Africa should monitor proposed changes closely and ensure that their views and interests are taken into account. West African governments may, for example, want to create a schedule of periodic consultations between EC officials and their own officials or officials of ECOWAS to review the implementation of directives for completing the EC and their probability effects on West Africa.

European Integration and the Economic Integration of ECOWAS

The Economic Community of West African States (ECOWAS) was formally launched in 1975 with the aim of creating an economic union among its 16 member states. The economic goals of ECOWAS were similar to those of the EC: to promote growth among member states by creating a market large enough to provide the economics of scale necessary for efficient production and to stimulate expanded trade and investment. Existing firms could expand their production and trade in an ECOWAS market of over 160 million people and potential investors would be encouraged to establish new firms to exploit that same market. Expanded trade in agricultural goods was to be encouraged, but the creation of ECOWAS was primarily a means of stimulating industrial trade and development.

ECOWAS is one of eight experiments in regional economic integration in sub-Saharan Africa today. (The others include the Communaute Economique de l'Afrique de l'Ouest, with seven West African countries as members; the Mano River Union among Liberia, Sierra Leone, and Guinea; the Union Douaniere des Etats de l'Afrique Centrale, with six African countries; the Communaute Economique des pays des Grands Lacs, among Zaire, Rwanda, and Burundi; the Communaute Economique des Etats de l'Afrique Centrale, including 10 countries; the Preferential Trade Area, with 14 countries of eastern and southern Africa; and the South African Customs Union, including Botswana, Lesotho, Swaziland, and the Republic of South Africa. The Southern African Development Coordination Conference (SADCC) has placed its emphasis on coordinating investment among its members rather than integrating the economies of its seven member states.) ECOWAS is one of the four subregional economic groupings in Africa that are a first step toward realizing the goal of the Lagos Plan of Action of creating a continentwide common market by the beginning of the twenty-first century. ECOWAS was established before the Lagos Plan of Action was signed at the Organization of African Unity meeting in Nigeria in 1980. The plan envisioned the creation of four subregional economic unions that would eventually be merged into one continentwide market by the year 2000. In addition to ECOWAS, the PTA and the CEEAC represent the other subregional groupings in sub-Saharan Africa that are part of the Lagos Plan.

ECOWAS was to achieve economic union in three successive stages. During the first (two-year) stage, members would freeze their tariffs on goods eligible from intra-ECOWAS trade. During the second (eight-year) period, members would eliminate their import duties on intra-ECOWAS trade. During a third stage, members would erect a common external tariff and eliminate other barriers to the free movement of goods, services, labor, and capital among themselves. An ECOWAS secretariat was set up to coordinate ECOWAS activities and an ECOWAS Fund was established to finance Community-wide projects and to provide compensation to those states suffering adverse economic effects from integration.

Unfortunately, ECOWAS has achieved relatively few of its goals thus far. Member states have supported policies to freeze and reduce tariffs on intra-ECOWAS trade but have failed to implement many of these decisions. By 1981 all member states were to have introduced the harmonized customs and trade documents. But, according to a 1983 assessment by the Economic Commission for Africa, no member state had done so. Nor does it appear that member states have begun to reduce their tariffs on imports from other members. Indeed, implementation of the trade liberalization protocol—the second stage of integration—has been delayed until 1990. Further, member states have been allowed to pay up their assessed contributions to the ECOWAS secretariat budget and to the capital of the ECOWAS Fund. Trade among ECOWAS member states has remained small—less than 5 percent of their total trade.

ECOWAS' disappointing performance has been of considerable concern to those many Africans and others that view the creation of economic unions, particularly among Africa's small states, as essential if the continent is ever to industrialize and achieve rapid growth. The ECOWAS failure is especially painful as the EC, long the model for experiments in economic integration throughout the world and especially for ECOWAS, promises to make rapid progress in completing the integration of its own market. Why has ECOWAS failed while the EC has been successful? And what can be done to turn ECOWAS' failure into success?

Discussions of the ECOWAS failure often point to the relatively short period of time it has existed, the economic problems, particularly the heavy debt burdens, of many member states, the passivity of the ECOWAS secretariat, and, above all, the "lack of political will" on the part of African leaders in implementing agreed integration policies. These are all very real problems, but they do not go far enough in explaining the disappointing performance thus far or what can be done to improve it in the future.

Behind the critical problem of a lack of political will, there are two sets of difficulties that distinguish ECOWAS from the EC and help explain its lack of progress. First are the economic difficulties. The two key member states of the original Economic Community—France and Germany—had diversified economics with different economic strengths. In the late 1950s when the EC was first established, both countries anticipated immediate economic benefits from reducing tariffs on trade between them. France looked forward to increasing its agricultural exports to Germany, and Germany expected to expand its manufactured goods exports to France.

The economies of ECOWAS member states, in contrast, are similar to one another. West African states produce and export mainly primary products, whereas they import manufactured goods. As a result, they have relatively little to exchange with one another in the short term, even if barriers to their trade are eliminated. The real benefits from economic integration to members of ECOWAS would come less from an immediate expansion in trade than from the new investment (foreign or domestic) that, it is hoped, will be stimulated by the creation of an enlarged market. But investment decisions are often slow to be made and implemented and are taken on the basis of the expected future profitability of the investment. Market size is only one element affecting the future profits, and not always the most important one. (Economic and political stability in the host country typically plays a far more important role in estimates of future profitability.) Thus the key benefits from economic integration among developing countries will usually be realized in the long run, if at all. The costs of integration, however, are often immediate. They can include: a drop in tax revenues resulting from a reduction in tariff barriers among member states, the failure of domestic manufacturing firms and ensuing increases in unemployment when such firms are unable to compete with cheaper imports from other member states, and an increase in the overall costs of imports if member states' imports shift from sources outside of Europe toward more expensive goods produced in other member states instead.

A key difference between the EC and ECOWAS is in the timing of potential costs and benefits. EC member states looked forward to immediate benefits that could in some measure offset the costs to them of economic integration. ECOWAS member states face the likelihood of suffering the costs of integration immediately and enjoying the benefits over the long term at best. Politicians rarely make decisions that carry immediate costs without the prospect of immediate benefits as well.

The economic differences between EC member states and ECOWAS members highlight another difficult problem that has challenged ECOWAS as well as other experiments in economic integration among developing countries. Whereas the economics of ECOWAS members are undiversified relative to those of EC members, the differences among them in their natural resource endowment, transportation, and communications facilities, degree of industrialization, and economic potential are considerable. Nigeria and the Cote d'Ivoire have already made a start on industrializing, even if that start is small compared to the degree of industrialization of EC member states. Their manufacturing sectors could benefit from an enlarged market. The smaller, poorer ECOWAS states—for example, Burkina Faso, Niger, Mali, Benin, or Togo—may not have the manufacturing firms that can take advantage of the larger ECOWAS market or manufacturing firms that do exist in those countries may face collapse if they cannot compete with Nigerian or Ivoirian goods. Moreover, Nigeria, Cote d'Ivoire, or Senegal, with their more developed infrastructure, including port, air transport, and communications facilities, are better situated to attract any new investments stimulated by market enlargement. In short, the benefits of integration, immediate and long term, may tend to concentrate in the few better-off member states, leaving the poorer states with only the costs. This is a well-known problem and one that contributed mightily to the breakup of the East African Community. It has been far less of a problem for the EC, though it has not been totally absent there either.

There are two ways to deal with this problem. One is to compensate the losers through direct financial transfers. The ECOWAS Fund was set up in part to fulfill this purpose. But compensation can be costly and become a constant source of tension as poorer states wrangle for larger transfers and better-off states resist such transfers. It is often difficult to set agreed levels of compensation, especially when such compensation is intended to offset the "costs" to poorer countries of not benefiting from new investments. And paying compensation remains especially difficult for governments of developing countries, all of which are strapped for money.

A second and even less satisfactory approach to the problem of the concentration of benefits of integration in a few countries is for member states of an integration agreement to direct new investments into poorer regions and countries through licensing requirements or subsidies and tax benefits. This has seldom worked and can actually discourage new investment.

There is yet another way of ensuring that poorer countries derive benefits from integration. That is permitting labor from those countries to migrate to the better-off, more rapidly growing member countries in an integration arrangement. Poorer countries that can export labor and receive remittances from better-off countries have an interest in the growth of those same countries and so are less likely to feel short-changed as new investment concentrates there. The patterns of trade and migration between the Cote d'Ivoire and several of its northern neighbors is one example of this type of exchange of benefits. However, with the many national, ethnic religious and political sensitivities throughout Africa, there has understandably been considerable resistance on the part of most countries to a free movement of labor among member states in economic integration schemes, including in ECOWAS. Indeed, the second phase in implementing a free movement of labor within ECOWAS had as of 1988 been ratified only by Senegal and Togo.

The second key difficulty distinguishing ECOWAS from the EC is the political environments in which the two different experiments were set up and have functioned. The EC was created among Western European countries in a Europe of the late 1950s, which was divided between East and West and where the threat of Soviet expansionism was still a fear. The creation of the North Atlantic Treaty Organization (NATO) was a political manifestation of this fear. But it was well recognized that economic strength would play a role in Europe's resistance to threats from the East and that by themselves European economies would probably be poorer and certainly politically weaker than if they were economically united. Economic union in Europe was also based on a desire to link important sectors of the German economy with the economies of West European countries to discourage a repetition of past conflicts. Another important political factor was the pressure and persuasion of the United States on the Europeans to move toward economic unity. As early as the Marshall Plan, the United States used its aid to Europe as a lever to encourage closer European economic cooperation, strengthening those Europeans, like Jean Monnet and Robert Schuman who were pursuing the vision of a united Europe. Thus the Europeans had strong political reasons and external political pressures on them to move toward economic integration.

There have been no external threats or pressures on ECOWAS countries equal to those on the Europeans to promote progress toward economic unity. The country that most exerted itself in supporting the establishment of ECOWAS was Nigeria. However, Nigerian diplomatic activism on behalf of ECOWAS lessened in the late 1970s as that country's leadership became absorbed with domestic political and economic challenges. In addition, during the period during which ECOWAS was created and began to function, there was at least a perception and perhaps the reality that France and some of the Francophone countries of West Africa were skeptical of the goals of ECOWAS.

It may well be that to achieve the very difficult goals of economic integration, member countries must be motivated by political as well as economic objectives. And external pressures can play an important political role in encouraging or discouraging progress toward integration.

One further point needs to be made regarding the differences between EC and ECOWAS in the achievement of economic integration. Success in one area of integration produces pressures for integration elsewhere. For example, the common agricultural policy of the EC has been relatively successful in creating EC-wide agricultural policies and an EC-wide market for agricultural commodities. But its very success has generated pressures for closer monetary cooperation among member countries. Completing the EC market in 1992 will likely exert yet more pressures toward monetary integration. A free movement of labor in the EC puts pressure on member states to harmonize their social policies. A free movement of capital puts pressure on them to adopt common fiscal policies. And so on. Getting started on implementing policies of economic integration may be the most difficult step in the entire process.

If these economic and political differences between the EC and ECOWAS explain why one organization has been relatively successful and the other relatively unsuccessful in achieving economic integration, what do they suggest about ways to promote more effective integration in ECOWAS in the future?

An Idea for Discussion

ECOWAS celebrates its fifteenth birthday in 1990. That anniversary, plus the implementation among an increasing number of ECOWAS members of trade liberalization measures and economic policy reforms as part of structural adjustment programs, suggest that the time may be propitious for a realistic assessment of past failures and a renewed effort by member states to make progress toward economic integration. But what can they do to make a new effort at integration any more successful than past efforts? How can they overcome the very real economic and political obstacles that have prevented progress toward integration in the past?

The rapid move by the EC toward completing its own market and the inspiration as well as the uncertainties that its progress has generated in Africa suggest that there is an opportunity for the EC to play a constructive role in supporting a renewal of efforts toward economic integration in ECOWAS. (See Tables 1–7 for statistical data on EEC/ECOWAS relationships.) An initiative by the EC in this area could also serve to reassure ECOWAS members as well as other developing countries that EC member states will remain sympathetic to the needs and interests of developing countries. The announcement by the EC of a special program of restructuring, reactivation, and strengthening for the Central American common market, supported by ECU 150 million dollars, shows that the Community has the

Table 1
Official Development Assistance from the EEC to West Africa
(Millions of $US)*

Country	1984	1987
Benin		
EEC	37.6	76.6
World	77.6	135.7
Burkina Faso		
EEC	86.4	168.3
World	188.6	283.1
Cote d'Ivoire		
EEC	112.7	233.4
World	127.8	253.7
Gambia		
EEC	21.7	41.0
World	53.6	103.5
Guinea		
EEC	38.9	94.6
World	132.2	214.0
Guinea (Bissau)		
EEC	25.2	36.4
World	55.2	104.4
Liberia		
EEC	21.3	22.2
World	133.2	78.4
Mali		
EEC	209.7	178.6
World	320.3	364.5
Mauritania		
EEC	50.5	89.2
World	175.0	177.7
Niger		
EEC	83.5	133.3
World	161.0	348.0
Nigeria		
EEC	13.8	33.3
World	33.0	69.3
Senegal		
EEC	155.2	317.9
World	368.0	642.1
Sierra Leone		
EEC	18.8	32.1
World	60.8	68.3

*Figures show disbursements of total ODA net.
Source: OECD, *Geographical Distribution of Financial Flows to Developing Countries*, Paris, 1989.

Table 8.5 *(handwritten)*

Table 2

ECOWAS Exports and Imports to and from the EEC (Millions of $US)

ECOWAS Members	Exports to EEC: 1981	1982	1983	1984	1985	1986	1987
BENIN	15	14	35	98	141	109	74
BURKINA FASO	24	23	16	30	34	52	69
CAPE VERDE	2	2	2	1	1	3	6
GAMBIA	14	17	30	26	12	14	37
GHANA	333	334	366	197	255	331	411
GUINEA	200	176	202	273	272	272	323
GUINEA-BISSAU	10	11	8	9	6	5	4
IVORY COAST	1499	1278	1163	1476	1783	1952	1805
LIBERIA	352	356	316	317	429	502	624
MALI	47	68	69	82	59	62	58
MAURITANIA	274	196	169	192	157	194	190
NIGER	212	233	233	179	173	216	369
NIGERIA	6665	6759	6839	7714	7975	4127	3120
SENEGAL	190	261	288	258	219	271	315
SIERRE LEONE	136	75	73	83	106	121	126
TOGO	128	99	83	120	106	144	116
TOTAL ECOWAS EXPORTS TO EEC:	10101	9902	9892	11055	11728	8375	7647

Table 8.4 *(handwritten)*

ECOWAS Members	Imports from EEC: 1981	1982	1983	1984	1985	1986	1987
BENIN	302	276	206	163	197	242	234
BURKINA FASO	170	168	129	102	134	221	214
CAPE VERDE	54	56	57	49	55	86	93
GAMBIA	59	54	54	49	62	88	102
GHANA	459	306	604	257	327	427	509
GUINEA	199	161	161	196	208	253	298
GUINEA-BISSAU	26	34	39	34	41	33	43
IVORY COAST	1211	1081	1016	822	927	1167	1260
LIBERIA	150	122	153	146	550	350	258
MALI	132	176	181	179	224	243	240
MAURITANIA	268	272	236	232	136	205	234
NIGER	245	210	169	153	190	184	192
NIGERIA	11294	8461	4720	3523	3747	3154	2906
SENEGAL	532	491	530	441	426	490	720
SIERRE LEONE	142	101	60	67	69	93	95
TOGO	285	244	175	172	228	326	339
TOTAL ECOWAS IMPORTS FROM EEC:	15528	12213	8490	6585	7521	7562	7737

Source: IMF Direction of Trade Statistics, 1988.

Table 3

A. Total ODA Gross from EEC to ECOWAS

	1984	1985	1986	1987
BENIN	6.6	5.1	10.7	12.0
BURKINA FASO	17.3	13.8	10.1	17.0
CAPE VERDE	7.6	3.0	10.7	6.3
GAMBIA	4.1	2.3	10.6	7.8
GHANA	46.5	11.5	39.5	11.8
GUINEA	13.9	8.2	12.9	13.1
GUINEA-BISSAU	8.9	6.5	6.1	11.1
IVORY COAST	11.3	9.3	44.6	27.8
LIBERIA	1.9	2.3	5.1	6.2
MALI	29.6	24.7	21.2	33.0
MAURITANIA	15.1	14.1	15.6	10.2
NIGER	16.1	27.5	27.4	18.6
NIGERIA	1.7	1.4	3.8	4.1
SENEGAL	20.8	6.2	64.8	74.4
SIERRE LEONE	5.7	8.2	5.8	4.7
TOGO	20.4	9.5	15.6	3.8
TOTAL ODA GROSS FROM EEC TO ECOWAS:	227.5	153.6	304.5	261.9

B. Total ODA Commitments from EEC to ECOWAS

	1984	1985	1986	1987
BENIN	8.7	16.4	12.6	42.6
BURKINA FASO	6.7	18.0	2.6	9.6
CAPE VERDE	11.9	0.1	6.7	5.9
GAMBIA	0.7	1.1	8.9	4.7
GHANA	34.0	13.2	31.9	57.0
GUINEA	26.8	13.4	7.4	98.8
GUINEA-BISSAU	11.0	8.4	6.2	32.3
IVORY COAST	6.9	4.9	50.2	47.4
LIBERIA	2.9	14.1	5.0	93.1
MALI	29.7	27.2	16.1	52.3
MAURITANIA	17.3	18.8	15.3	39.6
NIGER	43.5	21.3	18.6	63.4
NIGERIA	7.4	1.9	1.3	11.0
SENEGAL	17.6	3.1	70.3	194.0
SIERRE LEONE	5.2	3.0	11.5	29.5
TOGO	16.5	11.3	13.3	1.6
TOTAL ODA COMMITMENTS FROM EEC TO ECOWAS:	246.8	176.2	277.9	782.8

Source: OECD, Geographical Distribution of Financial Flows, 1989.

Table 4
A. Total Receipts Net from EEC to ECOWAS States: 1984–1987

	1984	1985	1986	1987
BENIN	6.5	5.1	10.5	11.8
BURKINA FASO	19.3	14.8	8.1	14.5
CAPE VERDE	7.6	3.0	10.7	6.1
GAMBIA	4.0	2.2	10.4	7.6
GHANA	45.7	11.5	37.8	10.0
GUINEA	13.5	10.4	15.0	13.3
GUINEA-BISSAU	8.9	6.5	6.1	11.1
IVORY COAST	3.2	4.0	37.4	39.7
LIBERIA	1.1	3.2	3.9	5.0
MALI	29.4	24.7	20.9	33.0
MAURITANIA	16.2	14.8	13.5	7.7
NIGER	16.6	27.5	25.9	17.3
NIGERIA	6.1	6.4	13.2	24.0
SENEGAL	22.4	6.6	62.7	70.6
SIERRE LEONE	5.7	8.2	5.8	4.7
TOGO	18.8	7.4	13.2	0.1
TOTAL RECEIPTS NET FROM EEC TO ECOWAS:	225.0	156.3	295.1	276.5

B. Total ODA Net from EEC to ECOWAS: 1984–87

	1984	1985	1986	1987
BENIN	6.5	5.1	10.5	11.8
BURKINA FASO	17.0	13.8	8.7	15.2
CAPE VERDE	7.6	3.0	10.7	6.1
GAMBIA	4.0	2.2	10.4	7.6
GHANA	46.4	11.5	39.4	11.8
GUINEA	13.9	8.2	12.9	13.1
GUINEA-BISSAU	8.9	6.5	6.1	11.1
IVORY COAST	9.8	9.3	42.5	25.7
LIBERIA	1.9	2.3	5.1	6.2
MALI	29.4	24.7	20.9	33.0
MAURITANIA	14.9	14.1	15.5	10.2
NIGER	16.1	27.5	27.4	18.6
NIGERIA	1.7	1.4	3.8	4.1
SENEGAL	20.7	6.0	64.8	73.9
SIERRE LEONE	5.7	8.7	5.8	4.7
TOGO	20.4	9.4	15.4	3.5
TOTAL ODA NET FROM EEC TO ECOWAS:	224.9	153.7	299.9	256.6

Source: OECD, Geographic Distribution of Financial Flows, 1989.

Table 5
Total Receipts and Total ODA Net from EEC Members of OECD*

	Total Receipts Net 1987	Total ODA Net 1987
BENIN	31.8	64.9
BURKINA FASO	146.0	153.2
CAPE VERDE	38.5	37.2
GAMBIA	36.1	33.4
GHANA	110.0	78.1
GUINEA	89.9	81.5
GUINEA-BISSAU	21.4	25.4
IVORY COAST	−52.9	212.2
LIBERIA	−59.7	16.0
MALI	139.1	145.6
MAURITANIA	72.4	79.2
NIGER	109.0	114.7
NIGERIA	511.8	29.3
SENEGAL	270.0	243.9
SIERRE LEONE	48.9	27.4
TOGO	51.9	68.2
TOTAL RECEIPTS NET AND ODA NET FOR 1987 FROM EEC MEMBERS OF OECD:	1564.2	1410.2

*Belgium, Denmark, France, Germany, Ireland, Italy, Netherlands, UK.

will and the funds to support integration efforts among developing countries. Can it do less for West African countries with which it has enjoyed such long and close political and economic relationships? Specifically, the EC could, together with member states of ECOWAS, develop a program of support (guarantees, direct loans, or grants) for integration in West Africa, a compact in which the EC would provide financial support for investments intended to exploit the entire ECOWAS market in exchange for trade liberalization within that market. It would be possible to focus such financial support on only specific sectors or types of production during a given period, for example, footwear or furniture, to encourage integration of those markets as a beginning toward broader trade liberalization and as a means of generating momentum and support for further progress toward integration. Together with support for investment, the EC could also provide support for infrastructure projects, to be undertaken in the poorer countries of ECOWAS, as a means of helping to compensate them where they are unable to enjoy the benefits of new investments and to improve their abilities to compete for investments in the future.

Table 6
Level of GNP and Population of ECOWAS in 1986 and Growth of
Real GNP and GNP per Capita 1976–86

Countries	GNP/CAP U.S.$ 1986	POP Millions 1986	Real Growth Rate GNP/ CAP %	Real Growth Rate GNP 76–86	1986 GNP U.S.$
BENIN	270	4.18	1.0	4.1	1380
BURKINA	150	8.1	0.6	3.0	1470
CAPE VERDE	450	0.34	4.5	6.4	160
GAMBIA	230	0.77	−2.5	0.8	170
GUINEA	290	6.32	−0.6	1.7	1540
GUINEA-BISSAU	170	0.9	−1.1	2.0	160
MALI	170	7.7	−0.6	1.9	1640
MAURITANIA	440	1.74	−0.1	2.0	750
NIGER	260	6.59	−0.8	2.1	2010
SIERRE LEONE	310	3.75	0.3	2.3	1140
TOGO	250	3.14	−1.1	1.8	940
GHANA	390	13.13	−1.8	1.1	5630
LIBERIA	450	2.28	−4.4	−1.2	1010
SENEGAL	420	6.77	−1.6	1.2	2840
COTE D'IVOIRE	740	10.43	−1.2	2.8	8850
NIGERIA	640	103.15	−4.1	−1.2	66210
		179.29			5993.75 w/o NIGERIA:
Average:	351.875	TOTAL	−0.84375	1.925	1979.333

Source: World Bank, as Taken from OECD *DAC Report,* 1988.

Table 7
Food Aid to Sub-Saharan Africa by EEC (Multilateral), 1982–86:
(Millions of $US)

	1982	1983	1984	1985	1986
	101	57	191	114	97
Area	75–76%	80–81%	85–86%		
SUB-SAHARAN AFR	58.4	60.1	55.9		
SOUTH ASIA	20.3	16.9	9.8		
OTHER ASIA	1.9	4.9	8.4		
MID EAST, N. AFR	14.1	11.8	12.7		
LATIN/CARIB	5.4	6.3	13.2		

Source: DAC Report, 1988.

The goals of ECOWAS will never be realized unless African political leaders want them to be and are willing to move forward toward economic integration. However, the obstacles to achieving integration remain daunting. An initiative by the EC providing material and moral support for a renewed effort at integration by ECOWAS members might help overcome those obstacles and set an example of hope and progress toward economic union among developing countries for the rest of Africa and the developing world.

4

STATEMENTS

Kenneth Dadzie
Secretary-General, UNCTAD

I agree with Carol Lancaster (Chapter 3) that "It is not clear at present what the economic impact of completing the EEC market will be on the rest of the world including the 16 countries of West Africa. Much will depend on what kind of Community-wide policies governing external economic relations are adopted as the remaining barriers to the free movement of goods, services, capital and labour among Community members are removed."

First, I address the possible impacts of EEC 1992 on trade linkages with West African countries. Perhaps the first point is that West African countries in the context of their diversification and aspirations are increasingly concerned to move toward increased production and export of manufactured and semimanufactured goods. The European Common Market will remain important for them for this reason, and if new regulations involving trade, health, or technical specifications governing imports of textiles and other such manufactures prove more restrictive than those currently in place, that market may prove more difficult to penetrate, possibly also discouraging investment in manufacturing for export from West Africa to the EEC countries. Thus the elimination of intra-EEC nontariff barriers may have little or insignificant effects on West African states because nontariff barriers within the Community do not apply to primary commodity exports. It nevertheless bears pointing out that it is an important part of EEC policy to leave to its member countries significant discretion to limit imports. I need only refer to the multifiber arrangement. Likewise subsidies other than those relating to the common agricultural policy are granted exclusively at the discretion of individual governments and members of the Community. Although this is not an aspect of the completion of the EEC market, it is worth remembering that individual governments can, notwithstanding the completion of the EEC market, take or continue measures that could have an adverse impact on the export trade of West African countries.

In the process of opening and liberalizing domestic markets, EEC countries have allowed a variety of barriers under national regulations to continue, barriers that clearly impede the freer flow of goods and services and take the form, for instance, of health and safety regulations, public procurement and sourcing policies of public enterprises, and so forth. Thus despite closer integration, individual country members of EEC could continue to place restraints on exports from West Africa through such nontariff barriers at the national level, possibly negating the beneficial effects of the EEC integration process itself.

Concerning the role and possible consequences of the Uruguay round, Lancaster has correctly pointed out that the possible outcome of the Uruguay round, particularly on agriculture, tropical products, natural resource-based products, and the level of preferences involved, could imply a wider range of benefits being extended to a much wider range in terms of developing countries. This could have a significant impact. I stress that this aspect of the matter needs to be continually kept in mind. The offers concerning the products just noted that are currently on the table as well as those to be negotiated cannot but affect the overall pattern of trade of West African countries, affecting not only the direction and composition of their future exports but also the degree of preferences presently enjoyed by them as a consequence of Lomé IV and GSP arrangements. If GSP and other preferences were to be extended to a wider range of developing countries, this would be a natural cause for concern by West African and indeed ACP states.

A third point is that if bilateral arrangements currently in force between EEC countries and West African countries were to be replaced by EEC-wide arrangements governing imports, for instance, with regard to bananas, textiles, footwear, and other products of export interest, a lot will hinge on whether such EC-wide arrangements are more or less restrictive.

Fourth, an important consequence of EEC integration process will hinge on the harmonization of the level of taxes on products using West African imports. It seems that if such harmonization were to result in an overall increase in taxes on goods or imports from West Africa, the demand for such imports may well fall, and vice versa.

Another point has to do with the possible harmonization of export credit facilities. If such harmonization will improve access to export credit, so much the better. But there is no guarantee that this will be the case.

As a result of the completion of the integration of the European market, output growth in the European Community may well grow at something like 0.5 to 1.5 percent above current levels. This clearly implies a larger market for a wider range of goods and services and an acceleration of the pace of investment and capital accumulation in the EEC. The extent to which West Africa can benefit from such a development will depend a great deal on the structural adjustment programs that West African countries are pursuing, by which I mean that such programs ought to permit a shift in the composition of exports if full advantage is to be taken of the increased vigor in the economies of the EEC. This is, of course, linked to the outcome of Lomé IV and the Uruguay round. But it would call for a pattern of investment and trade that would capture, as indicated, the benefits of an expanded and more homogeneous European market.

Let us turn to rules of origin. It is worth pointing out that there has been friction between the EEC and ACP countries in the past, particulary as concerns EC practices on rules of origin. In the view of ACP countries, these practices have been a considerable impediment in the way of effective utilization of the free access provisions of the Lomé Conventions. In this area, as in others, it remains to be seen whether the Community post-1992 does become less or more protectionist.

Finally, again on the issue of trade linkages, one cannot ignore the evolution of the common agricultural policy. The CAP is widely considered to have exerted an important influence on the trade practices of a number of agricultural products, some of them of great importance to countries in West Africa. The impact of an evolution in CAP would center on the terms of trade with EEC; clearly, countries that compete with EEC's own agricultural products, whereas those exports that do not compete with EEC would benefit because of the lower prices of imported food and increased demand from Europe for substitutes for high-priced domestic agricultural products.

Furthermore, the liberalization that we hope will take place in CAP beyond 1992 might induce developing countries to get into the production of temperate zone commodities locally and may contribute to a switch in these countries from net importers to exporters. Whether in fact CAP will be liberalized or reformed in the wake of the Uruguay round and in the context of the generalized move toward deregulation remains to be seen. But it will have a clear impact on the trade performance of the West African states. The membership of Portugal and Spain the EEC suggests that two concentrations need to be watched. First, their links to Latin American countries may result in pressures to extend EEC preferences to a wider set of countries. Second, given the relatively weak economic position of these two countries, they will have to face the temptation to restrain further liberalization of the EEC market in products of export interest to them.

In conclusion, it seems that the long-run impact on West African countries of the completion of the EEC market is likely to be more significant than the short-run implications. Whether this long-run impact will be positive or negative will depend, among other things, on the implications for commodity prices and terms of trade. Obviously if economic growth were to pick up as we project in the EEC, this could be translated into increased demand for West African exports, particularly minerals and agricultural raw materials that are used in industrial production. With regard to the financial aspects, EC 1992 might, and indeed will in my opinion, stimulate investment in EC. But it is not at all clear to what extent this might serve to reduce the flow of investment in West Africa. EC 1992 might also stimulate capital flows toward southern Europe and the Maghreb countries, and the question arising is whether this will be at the expense of West African nations as would be the greater diversification of EDF concessional flows to other developing countries.

The question has also been raised about the future of the Union Monetaire of West Africa. Clearly if the franc zone were to be dissolved or if it were to disintegrate, this could have devastating effects on the economics of the countries that are currently members. But equally it could serve as a possible stimulus by virtue of the fact that one barrier, at least one factor that is considered by many nonmember countries as a barrier to ECOWAS integration, will thereby have been removed.

I conclude with a quotation from Dr. Herbert Onitiri, who says, "It is not an accident that the world is witnessing a renewed interest in the formation and consolidation of trading blocks, at a time that negotiations are in progress in the Uruguay round for movement towards freer trade. The apparent contradiction has been variously interpreted. One view is that it reflects a sobre assessment of what can be achieved in the current negotiations and a recognition that the relentless march of technology will continue to put a premium on economic size and on the capacity to adjust as rapidly as possible to changing situations in world markets. This situation has to be taken into account if developing countries are not to be left further behind in the technology driven world of the future." He adds that "This gives added force, if such additional force were needed, to the argument that West African countries should devote far more political commitment and political will to the integration movement in West Africa than they have hitherto done."

--------◆•◆◀------

Adrian Hewitt
Deputy Director, Overseas Development Institute, London

There is considerable interest in the impact of 1992 on developing countries, not just in the appropriate ministries—the Department of Trade and Industry and the Foreign Office, etc.—but also among the legislature. Some months ago, a group I organize in the House of Commons, the all-party parliamentary group on overseas development, had a session on this topic. It is partly because if you look at the 1985 white paper, the more glamorized Cecchini Report, even our own British Department of Trade and Industry glossary on the effects of 1992—completing the internal market, there is no mention anywhere of the actual or predicted effects on developing countries as such. To some extent this is natural; the market that wants to integrate itself further is going to look at the effects on itself. But there has been a lack of research in predicting and specifying the effects on developing countries and warning those governments what action they should take to preserve or strengthen their position. In contrast, when I talk to businessmen in the Community, the position is much further advanced already. They assure me that from their trading point of view, 1992 was here long ago and they are operating and doing deals on that basis.

Let us briefly review the nuts and bolts of the timetable for 1992. Effectively it is just three things: removal of physical, technical, and fiscal barriers to completing the internal market. Let me give examples of each as they will affect African developing countries and West African products or countries, wherever it is possible to be specific in that respect. Concerning the physical barriers—in a sense there should be no physical barriers anyway as the Community has been in existence for some decades now. Where there are physical barriers on products affecting developing countries, one can classify them into two cases: barriers that have been set up to help often for reasons of past history.

Secondly are barriers that clearly do not help, such as on textiles. On bananas and rum, that is a fait accompli. The market for bananas will be completely liberalized as of 1992 and the Windward Islands can sink into the sea—these are the implications for countries such as Somalia and Cote d'Ivoire, which have special deals with Britain, France, and Italy. It does not seem that the Commission has conceded the fact that the market is going to be completely deregulated by 1992. A lot of effort is going on precisely to do that, if not preserve the position of particularly dependent banana exports effectively against dollar bananas (Latin America). There is also a lot of work to be done on the countervailing or compensatory measures to be put in place if this issue is going to be conceded. But it is my understanding that the issue has not been conceded yet. That surely is very important for the banana producers. Rum is not so interesting for West Africa except perhaps in its consumption. Textiles is a completely different case. The multifiber arrangement is one of the trade regulations, the arrangements for managing trade, for preventing a free market in goods, which actually discriminate against developing countries. There are not a lot of these. Within this arrangement it has country quotas. Individual member states of the EEC are to stay within their quotas and there is not supposed to be an internal trade in MFA-imported products within the Community, although of course a lot of this does go on. By now some sort of agreement might have been expected, especially with the GATT round preceding, and this present multifiber arrangement, which expires in 1990, would be the last, and therefore the whole issue by 1992 would not be relevant.

Now, on to technical barriers. The problem we have as a research institute in producing results in our studies of the effects of 1992 on developing countries is that when we are dealing with technical and physical barriers, nobody knows as of now, even though there is a calendar for achieving things by 1 January 1993, whether technical standards, labor standards, or fiscal harmonization is going to go up or down. The answer probably is that in certain cases it will go up and become tougher or it will become more beneficial, and in other cases it will go down and become weaker. One has to be well informed about the issues. There is no alternative to that and there are no simple solutions. Let us take some cases of technical barriers that can include; health standards, labor conditions, etc. A technical barrier that would be of the most interest to West Africa is the use of fats in the production of chocolate. In some Community countries, probably Belgium and France, there are restrictions on the sort of products you put with cocoa in the production of chocolate. You can only use cocoa butter; you can't use any cheap noncocoa-based vegetable oils, whereas in England the consumers have developed a taste for this; over the years you put in other products. If the standards are raised upward to the tough French level, that would mean more demand for cocoa products. It would mean that the British type of chocolate could not be called chocolate anymore; it would be called vegelate. All these things would have an effect on the demand for raw materials and, to some extent, the processed products that West African countries produce. The same could apply to an obscure product such as vanilla. The standards for the use of vanilla in ice cream and food flavorings, etc. are much higher in France than in Britain. The standards could go up or they could be lowered.

One last issue on technical barriers is the question of aircraft noise. Ultimately those standards are going to be raised; there is no question of lowering the standards of noise. Therefore the countries that have national airlines already financially strapped or regional, multinational airlines will not be permitted to fly into any Community airports if the standards are raised. They would have to think seriously about their investment programs and policies.

The third area is fiscal harmonization. Some member states think that there is no reason for this to be complete and absolute. The actual numbers of value-added tax or excise tax don't have to be same, but there has to be a movement toward similarity of treatment. However, it could go anywhere along that line. The matter at issue is principally indirect taxes VAT on purchases and excise taxes at the European Community front because some of these taxes are inordinately high by general Community standards in countries such as Denmark and Germany on cocoa and coffee compared to France and Belgium. A reasonable supposition would be that by 1992 harmonization could mean a reduction in those very high tariffs and therefore a stimulus to demand for coffee and cocoa in the countries that are high in direct tax areas.

The major force in 1992 conveyed by its proponents is that it is going to create not only a more integrated market but a better market with stronger growth. Kenneth Dadzie noted a conservative range of 0.5 to 1.5 percent growth as a result of completion of the internal market. That is appreciable anyway if you add it to whatever growth one is getting already. But figures range up to an extraordinary 7 percent in European GNP suggested as a result of the completion of the internal market. Let me, however, add a word of caution. It does not necessarily mean that if any of these figures were the real ones that all or any of this would be transmitted to a demand for extra goods and services from the outside world or from developing countries in particular. In fact, the basic theory about customs union talks about two separate issues: trade diversion and trade creation. It is normal to suppose that at least one important reason for the wish of the European Community to integrate itself further is to divert trade that previously was import-export trade into the internal market. So it is only the trade creation aspects of the process that are, in the first round, directly beneficial to developing countries and to Third World countries. These might be quite minor. I concede that the effects of the second round of a more prosperous and efficient Community market would then generate other growth effects. It is these second round effects that must have been heavily written into the 7 percent growth figures I came across. The locomotive effect is principally within Europe. Investment opportunities could have some beneficial effects on developing countries if they are aware of the issues at hand. This can work on both outward and inward investment. Let me give one example of such an issue, which has been triggered by the process of completing the internal market. It comes not from West Africa but from South America whose countries do not have the same long-term trading and investment relationship with Europe. The investment relationship tends to be in the other direction. Brazil is already establishing industrial companies in Portugal, which is also a low-wage area just to make sure that it finds itself inside the Community rather than outside if the threat of fortress Europe were to materialize.

There are other issues that are even more important. First is the monetary union. Sometimes it seems to be in and sometimes it seems to be out. A short time ago, monetary union had a big setback. I am sure it will recover in time, but 1992 is not the timetable that will apply to monetary union. In contrast, the possible dissolution of the franc zone does mean that sort of area of monetary affairs is moving much faster than one would have anticipated, say, three years ago. The franc zone itself is a matter for deep thought and considerable revision.

On labor standards, human rights, and immigration, these are not properly economic issues but they pertain to them. There is a complete range of laws that could have applied to these until about a year ago. There is the Loi Pasqua in France, while in Britain there are special concerns about Hong Kong, and policies are being deliberated and changed at this moment. This is a very difficult area that could not possibly come into the fairly straightforward removal of the barriers in the Community.

Last is one area that should properly be in the 1992 portfolio but isn't— the harmonization of aid. This must be of particular interest to West African countries. The situation is that there is one Community aid program to which all the member states contribute and there are, if not 12, nearly 12 bilateral aid programs. Additionally, all the member states contribute to the aid programs of others, notably of the international financial institutions and UN organizations. I do not think very much will change on the third element, although obviously if the proportions change that is one that could well be squeezed. The main issue is whether the member states of the Community should have bilateral aid programs as well as having a Community aid program. Everybody can envisage that at some time in the future it would make sense to have a Community aid program, perhaps in isolation, but we are very far from that and I don't think we are talking about 1992 in these terms. However, let us think about it logically. If public procurement were to be harmonized, if the procedures for public procurement were to be fully integrated within the Community and restrictions on public procurement for goods and ultimately services within an individual nation state were to be removed, there would be a certain lack of logic for not requiring that that happen also to the public procurement that happens to be spent outside the Community's borders. Therefore, if you were to believe that the main purpose behind bilateral aid programs is to be a vector for the export promotion of the goods and services of the individual national donor, the importance of that would begin to erode, to put it mildly, and in future one would be talking about the promotion of goods and services from Europe rather than from individual member states. So certainly in the medium to long term, I can see a weakening of the trade-based rationale for national and therefore bilateral aid programs in favor of a stronger Community aid program. In the same way that Kenneth Dadzie noted export credit and export credit guarantees, logically and even by 1992 it would be logical not to have individual export credit agencies (ECGD, HERMES, etc.) competing against each other for the best deals and the best rates and come to argue in the OECD-Development Assistance Committee about it. In due course there should be a European export credit agency that would be stronger.

There are issues happening in the context of the 1992 program that are almost as important as the nub of the matter itself. On the issue of structural adjustment and Lomé IV, the European Community is in an acute dilemma and it is going to affect the aid relationships that African countries, and West African countries in particular, have with the Community. To put it at its simplest, the issue is that whereas the World Bank and the IMF have very firm policies on structural adjustment and on supplying aid from their institutions in exchange for prescribed policy reforms, the European Community has not gone along with that. The Community has been much more happily attuned to project aid and has conceded that there needs to be a balance now of program aid and project aid in countries with severe macro economic difficulties. But so far, and I think correctly, the Community has not said that all we do is to accede to the World Bank and IMF conditionalities and supply additional money to strengthen them. After the Lomé IV negotiations are completed, the Commission is going to have to have a stronger view. I do not think it will go wholeheartedly in with the World Bank and IMF. There will be no rationale for that at all. But it can't stay completely outside. It cannot say that it will treat countries without adjustment programs in the same way as those that do, and we are not going to exercise any political intervention in those countries that won't change their policies, which are a drain on the balance of payments of the world and indeed which are a drain on the balance of payments of one of our key member states, which is France.

The three dilemmas I see are, first, will the Community get itself into a position where it has to withhold its own aid from countries because they refuse to agree to a program with the Bretton Woods institutions? Some of these are actually in West Africa, Sierra Leone, Liberia, Benin, and Ethiopia—not in West Africa but a case in point. Until now the Lomé Convention has been run, at least on the surface, with a respectable degree of apoliticism, nonpolitical intervention, which is why you have Ethiopia and Gabon in the same grouping. The EEC will be in a position where it will have to challenge the World Bank and IMF and say that whereas they might be withholding their aid, they may be encouraging individual bilateral donors to withhold their aid from countries like Benin, Sierra Leone, etc. They might find that some member states, my own government included at the moment, would tend to take the Washington line on this. There is a real dilemma where to go next.

The second dilemma is almost as acute. Because project aid at least has a certain amount of collateral behind it, you are building a dam and even if it isn't a very good dam, you still have the dam at the end and maybe you can get something back from it. The only collateral you have in policy-based lending is the success of the political change. If you don't succeed there is nothing to show for the stream of imports you financed. That is dangerous in its own right. Because in addition money that is not attached to projects becomes that much more fungible; it can trickle down into all sorts of unexpected areas. The EEC or any donor could find itself in an awkward position, if it goes along with the Washington lead on policy-based lending, on structural adjustment. It could find itself in the position of effectively helping to maintain the interest payments on return loans to the IMF. That is not a very comfortable position to be in. All the member states of the European Community as donors and lenders meet in the Paris Club. They agree to reschedule, they agree maybe to bring extra money forward, and increasingly they will be agreeing to write off some of their past loans to developing countries; and to Africa in particular. But at the moment the World Bank and the IMF, legally according to their articles of association, cannot reschedule and they cannot write off any past loans. Again, there is a conflict there.

Last, the whole issue of structural adjustment lending brings to the European Community the question of whether it is going to remain an agent for development. A previous EC commissioner for development, Edgar Pisani, has said that the Lomé Convention was made for development and to confuse it with adjustment is a confusion of terms. There are alternatives being generated against the World Bank/IMF approach to structural adjustment, especially in Africa. At the beginning one looked rather desperately for alternatives, but now many are emerging. The report of the ECA begins to make an alternative proposal. UNICEF has been very successful, concentrating on the welfare and consumption aspects of adjustment. It has made a very successful bid and has influenced the IMF and World Bank successfully in this direction. In Helsinki the UNU Wider-World Institute for Economic Research has begun to produce an alternative program.

Obviously the GATT round is another element that should be seen in the context of 1992. Third World debt issues are exceedingly important. We are beginning to see a two-track approach attempting to resolve the issue of outstanding debt, one for the very large middle-income debtors, essentially the Western Hemisphere and Philippines and one or two others, and another for Africa. I am not sure where Nigeria and Cote d'Ivoire fit into that, whether they fit into the African category or the mega-debtors. This is crucial because there is going to be a much more concessionary approach from the public authorities to the African approach and much more pressure placed on the banks to write off. One has to be very aware of politics.

Dieter Frisch

Director General for Development
Commission of the European Communities

I focus here on the strictly 1992 aspects that have been raised by preceding contributors. Martin Bangeman (Chapter 2) gave the general thrust of our approach to partners outside the Community in the perspective of 1992.

Some of the ideas and elements, if they were expressed by a group of South-east Asian countries, would have more relevance than expressed within a group of African countries. First of all, within the Lomé arrangements at present and within the future ones, there is no risk of having the European market closed in any way. The idea of a kind of differentiation in the West African trade regime with the Community market between commodities and manufactures is simply wrong. It is a basic principle of the Lomé Convention and it will remain a basic principle of the future that West Africa have free access to the Community market. There is not even a restriction on textile exports, for example, Mauritius, which largely benefits from that, exports without restrictions to the Community. There are a few restrictions left, but they are marginal in terms of West African trade. There are a few agricultural products with perhaps 1 to 2 percent maximum of the bulk of African trade with the Community that come in some conflict with the European agricultural policy, perhaps strawberries, beans, etc., not products that are really relevant. They are relevant, however, to some of the countries; Kenya is doing a good deal of business with green beans, for example. But there is nothing important as an obstacle that is presently left over.

Second, the idea that in 1992 we would change in terms of more protection is certainly not relevant. Some points of Kenneth Dadzie and Adrian Hewitt (earlier this chapter) are important in this respect. Of course, there are presently a certain number of quantitative national restrictions left over for a few products—exactly nine cases for ACP countries. These restrictions must disappear. National restrictions that would limit the free circulation within the Community are not compatible with 1992, so these national restrictions must disappear.

As far as West African countries are concerned, the few quantitative restrictions that remain are very likely to disappear. This is a positive point. I do not see new restrictions coming up at the common border of the Community. A specific case is bananas, which as presently organized is incompatible with 1992 because the Community market is segmented into four or five pieces, and free circulation in 1992 is incompatible with the present arrangement. But Hewitt raised the question of whether we have abandoned the idea of maintaining the advantages of our present special partners. In our negotiations with the Lomé countries, we have clearly stated that the present arrangements are incompatible so we will have to draw up a new technical device. We have taken a commitment in the negotiations that any future regime would maintain the objectives of the present arrangements. This means we must find a technical device to sustain and help our traditional banana importers from the countries (Caribbean more than Africa) that are not competitive with the dollar banana.

Then there is the other area of standards and norms. There is no general move toward harmonization. We started some years ago with the idea that technical standards have to be harmonized in the Community and we got deeply into difficulties with that process, which would never have ended, certainly not by 1992 and probably not by 2000. The present approach is that norms are only harmonized in some of the sensitive areas, which touch public health, environmental matters, etc. The principle, on the contrary, is mutual recognition of one or the other country. What is legally produced in one country must be accepted in the other country. So this also means for those who come into the Community, into any of its border places, if their product is compatible with the law of that country, then it must be accepted by the rest of the Community, even if the rules in the other countries are different. In cases (such as the fat chocolate case) there was an attempt two or three years ago to harmonize that. There is always a risk that when you harmonize, you take the easy way. To accommodate everybody you take the one that is the easier. So there was a risk that we would harmonize chocolate on the British level. Now this has been abandoned and the principle is mutual recognition of norms. So the one who produces the better chocolate just has to make enough promotion and labeling and convince the consumer that one is chocolate and another is a different foodstuff. The same is true of the vanilla case. As far as harmonization is necessary, we are committed. It is the only case in the world that I know where we are committed to inform our partners of any change we are starting to prepare and that is likely to affect their interests. We inform them, we consult them, and we suspend our legislation until this consultation process is over. I don't think there is any other case in the world where a group of industrial countries or an industrial country suspends its legislation to take into account the views and interests of its farmers. As regards the cadmium contents in phosphates that are dangerous, we have a discussion about harmonizing the norms, but we have associated our colleagues from Senegal and Togo closely. Of course, sometimes there are conflicting interests. If we do something in cadmium, it is not as a trade barrier, it is because the public health concerns in Europe become so strong that we have to take that into account. Sometimes there is a conflict between the objective of trade development and the objective of protecting public health. You have to find a compromise somewhere in the middle. You will never have just one objective to be pursued and the other be completely neglected.

Kenneth Dadzie suggested that our member countries would be allowed to maintain national subsidies. We have very strict rules in the Community about subsidies. The Rome Treaty allows only subsidies that are compatible and are not doing harm to the competition within the Community. So there is not at all the freedom for member countries to subsidize their economies as they want. They have to notify each case and it can only be done if it is compatible with the competition rule of the Common Market.

A short word on harmonization in the fiscal field. We are not very advanced there. It is very difficult to say what kind of effects this will have—positive or negative. The effect might be rather neutral for African affairs. As far as the rules of origin are concerned, again a subject of discussion in our Lomé negotiations, I could say that in our judgment our ACP partners attach more importance to the rules of origin than they really have for their trade development. One of the examples we normally quote is that we have rules of origin, but we have the possibility of derogations. Any country that does not fulfill the normal rules can apply for derogation. The strange fact is that in the course of one Lomé Convention—five years—we have perhaps two or three cases where a derogation from these basic rules was asked for. But the ACP countries say that this is a kind of potential obstacle, because if these rules were not there investors would come more easily. We have to discuss that, but we must also know that a minimum of value added in the countries themselves is of economic importance for themselves. West African countries don't want to become just transit countries, where a product from somewhere comes in, is wrapped in a piece of paper and sent to the Community, saying it is originating from Nigeria or one of the other African countries. This leaves nothing for the African economy and just creates a kind of diversion of trade. Some reasonable degree of value added is not only a claim we have, but it is also in the interest of African development. There is no use in having just a superficial kind of industrialization.

A word on the agricultural policy. For the last two or three years our reform program for the agricultural policy is serious. We have been talking about it for many years and things have really started to work. Price decisions have been taken by our agricultural ministers that are on the restrictive line and will create a lot of unease within the agricultural community of Europe. But the fact is there. We are moving in the right direction. We used to be surplus producers of dairy products. There is no dairy surplus anymore, although a few years ago we had a million tons of butter in our stores. It is adjusted. We are adjusting in other areas. For the time being there are still surpluses in some areas and you could say that our products with their export subsidies come to the African coast at cheaper prices than Africa's own production costs. If that is so, West African sovereign countries have the right to protect their markets against anything that disturbs their economies. When we had problems in some of the countries where we wanted to support irrigated agricultural production—rice in the whole of the Sahel area—there was a conflict. Not with our rice but with Southeast Asian rice, which is on the market much cheaper than the production cost in Niger or the Sahel countries. We had discussions with the World Bank and we have agreed that in such a case, liberalization as a basic principle must be moderated to make the country use its agricultural potential and to protect its market to a certain degree. I don't know why we should apply absolutely pure market economies in African countries when the same principle is moderated in all our countries here, although we are firmly committed to the market economy. This is also a personal statement.

As far as trade is concerned, the real problems of trade performance in Africa, and in West Africa in particular, are in our judgment not the trade access regime to the Community. The real problems are structural in African countries. They are the problem of the competitivity of African countries on our markets. It is a fact that despite the preferential regime Africa has on our market, for some traditional products Africa has lost market shares in favor of some of the Southeast Asian countries that have not the same degree of access. There is some protection, but they are more aggressive in terms of trade. There is a problem of competition and of getting the structures right. This is why structural adjustment, at least in that context, is relevant as far as getting African structures back on a healthy basis. There is a clear hope that a better performance can be obtained. It is also relevant that African structures are not just put in order on the national level but that they are also approached and put in order on the regional level. This is the basic problem.

The second problem that is real and has been referred to is what our ACP partners call the erosion of preferences. This is what Dadzie referred to concerning the Uruguay round, when he discussed GSP. It is true that as the major trading partner in the world, the Community must participate and wants to participate in international trade negotiations. So we play our part in the Uruguay round. It is mathematically true that the more one liberalizes with everybody, the better GSP one offers to all developing countries, the lower the margin that is maintained for those that come in at zero. We try, but it is not easy, to keep a fair balance in this approach. For the really sensitive products of the African countries, we try to make our proposals in Geneva such that they accommodate major African concerns. But we cannot do it on the whole line because it would mean that it would stop the whole trade negotiations from our side and protect exclusively the interests of the African countries. There is another point. In these negotiations, the African countries should better defend their interests. This presents a dilemma in Geneva because African nations are in solidarity with the group of developing countries asking for liberalization. Sometimes African nations want us to defend their special interests in the GATT negotiations where they have a tendency to join the developing countries as a group and ask for something that is contrary to what is being asked from us. These are the two areas where I see a real problem, the structural problem and the relative preferential situation on our markets.

There will be in the Community one point of risk, that the open, larger market will be a market with stronger competition. There we have to see that the weaker countries among our partners have the occasion to seize the opportunities that are offered. We are ready to help our partner countries with technical assistance and investment to adapt themselves to the new conditions and use them.

Finally, a word about financial and technical aid. Private capital is a subject in Lomé IV negotiations and will certainly have new and I hope more operational rules in the next Lomé Convention. But whatever we do as public bodies, governments, and ourselves, there is a need to create the incentives from both sides and to make West African countries attractive for private capital. There again, I think it is a question of structural adjustment. If the countries of West Africa can start on a new basis and put order in their economies, then automatically there will be a stronger attraction for private capital. Ghana, which is still in difficulties but is going through the adjustment process with a good deal of success, seems now to be strongly attracting capital from the private sector in the Netherlands, for example. There is not necessarily a disengagement of European capital in these countries as far as the conditions/framework is there, but there is good hope that things can start anew. As far as public finance is concerned, there is no risk that the EDF will be diluted. We have historically shown that the EDF, which is technically linked to the Lomé Convention, has been steadily increasing. It is true that we have increased our aid to Asia and Latin America, but we have not done it in the past and will not do it in the future to the detriment of the Lomé financial package. I hope that in the ongoing negotiations we will obtain a fair deal.

Adrian Hewitt's remarks about 1992 and possible developments in the aid field are very relevant. For example, I do not share the view (and neither does he) that there is scope for thinking that the Community will take over completely the bilateral aid program. We have to live with the situation of a peaceful coexistence and complementarity of the bilateral aid programs and the Community aid programs. But the past has shown that the Community aid program has relatively grown, and 1992 is relevant for a better coordination and a better complementarity and coherence between the national aid programs and the Community aid program. We are working very hard on that and have good achievements in the last few years. I would also say with much prudence that tieing or untieing bilateral aid may be relevant to 1992. We have not checked that completely.

The last point is on monetary matters. If one follows the work in the Community about monetary and economic union, the Delors report indicates that we are moving forward. But there is no dramatic speed. We certainly need a good deal of time to come to that point. At this juncture, speculations about the franc zone, etc. are really premature and are kind of a futuristic debate. If we come to the monetary union and if the countries want to have their links maintained either with this future money or with one of the Community monies, I do not see a mechanical or technical link that would impede that. I see no risk there, at least not in my generation.

The Community's position on structural adjustment is that we are serious on the reform support. We are doing it in the sectoral area now. Nobody has talked to Ethiopia about pricing policies and liberalization of marketing other than ourselves. If there are results there and if they are due to a dialogue with somebody, it will be due to the Commission of the European Communities. We are in close contacts with our colleagues in Washington. We have a very good relationship with the World Bank and with the IMF. Our position is not to draw up a kind of parallel contrast program; we must come together in the policy advice we give, in the dialogue with the country. So we will not subordinate our positions to the Washington institutions; we want to have a partnership dialogue with the countries and with the Washington institutions to put our policy advice on a common line. This is the objective we are pursuing. A better structured Community has been and will remain a positive element in North-South relations. If the Community had not had one voice at the Toronto summit, the arrangements would not have been drawn up. There is an interest for developing countries to have the Community grow, and it is not to grow to the detriment of our partners.

Comments

Olusegun Obasanjo. Dieter Frisch said that access to market is not our problem. I go along with that to a large extent. Maybe part of our problem, if not the whole of our problem, is the performance in that market, which he also noted. To some extent it means we are not putting our house in order. But in areas where we have even attempted to put our house in order, price stability has become another problem. Where we have access to the market, the prices we get out of the market have really made things difficult for us. To my mind, concerning structural adjustment and the policy of liberalization, it appears that what we get on one hand, we lose on the other. These are some of the things about which we will see how we can solve these apparent contradictions. The Community should also take cognisance not only of access to market but of stability in price.

Nan Nguema. Will the opening up of the Common Market in 1992 not lead African countries to revise their strategies, coming back to what we should have been doing right from the start rather than what we have been doing hitherto? On the question of access to the market, in Dieter Frisch's view that is not a problem. He says that the real problem for us is the ability to move within the market. I think one could agree with that provided, of course, we have the means to respond as most companies in Europe do. These large companies can offer their goods and services in the market at price levels generating profits for them.

On Support to ECOWAS

The European Community is a group of countries trying to integrate, and it is only normal for us to feel particularly called upon to support any cooperation initiatives on the part of developing countries. At times we dare to hope that we are stimulating this because of the challenge we represent. A representative of the ASEAN countries told me that the reason for its formation was partly due to our request not to have to talk separately with each of the countries, thereby encouraging them to group together. This is the sort of approach we use whenever possible.

Lomé is very much part of our approach. However, regional cooperation both in Africa and Europe must remain at a size that is manageable. Of course, it is very difficult to get support for regional cooperation, much more difficult than the traditional form of assistance to each country. If we look at the regional funding—there is a special fund of about 1,000 million ECU, which is there to support interstate cooperation—it amounts to about 40 percent. For West Africa, the performance of regional cooperation measured on that basis is not very good. The performance seems to be better in southern African where we have SADCC implementing the regional program which is at virtually the same level of progress as the national levels. It is also good in eastern Africa but less good in other regions. To be quite honest if we run through the various Lomé Conventions it is the African countries that asked us to help them. In Lomé I they asked us to put all our funds into regional cooperation, but after that it was up to us to push for a specific amount to be allocated to regional cooperation because there is a trend to opt for the easiest course, which is the trend to opt for individual countries. That is a lesson we can draw.

But we must not conclude that we should lose courage because of this. If we find that above all in Africa regional cooperation is something that is economically vital, we must give support for that despite the practical problems, even if we are subsequently criticized because of the slower liberalization of financial funds. If we look at the political will, this is something that is absolutely vital. At times it seems there must be external political pressure for a group to get really organized. The fact that southern Africa is working well is partially due to the political context of these countries that are condemned to cooperate more than a more peaceful region. To draw the parallel of Europe, we can say we needed to have the war and perhaps the cold war to lead us to being our own process of integration.

Another thing we have found is that cooperation is not facilitated in regions where there is a proliferation of regional organizations. I think that West Africa is in the front line here because you have ECOWAS, CEAO, CILSS, and many other organizations with particular tasks. I am not saying we cannot live with these organizations, we can, providing they work in a compatible way. As an external partner, in an area such as West Africa it is difficult to find the one partner. In southern Africa we have a partner, one single entity with which we can discuss our regional cooperation program. In West Africa the many entities are in rivalry with each other, they are not the specific entity appointed by these countries to negotiate on their behalf. This is why for cooperation in West Africa we have tried to promote ministerial conferences to push for regional cooperation and define priorities. We would advise a pragmatic approach, step by step. Do not fall into the trap of having excessive ambitions. If you look at the history of the Community, you will see that you have to do things that are feasible and politically right at the time. Paradoxically this is not necessarily one of things that is in the treaty. We have had to update the Treaty of Rome with the Single Act of 1987 because it was in some areas out of date. But in the meantime we did a number of things that were not included in the treaty, and curiously enough we had not done some things that were included in the original treaty. The treaty gives us a mandate to draw up a common transport policy, but this still does not exist 30 years later. The treaty says nothing about the environment and development and yet, because the time was politically right, we have done this. The treaty said nothing before the Single Act about political cooperation, but this emerged by itself when economic development ministers felt the need to discuss politics as well. You must do things that are within easy reach and not aim at things in the distant future.

Another comment from our experience with regional organizations. Generally speaking, these organizations are tempted by highly visible projects; less spectacular matters that are more essential such as promoting integration are precisely the tasks they put to one side. Often they prefer to finance a road—you don't need a regional organization to do this. This was the case of the PTA recently who came to discuss with us roads in Kenya, etc. I said that it was their task to organize regional trade, and roads could be taken care of by the countries. In our negotiations on the future Lomé Convention, we want to concentrate on this type of integration and we want to be careful not to finance from the regional funds projects that are not priorities. This is another temptation. Countries tend to present the real priorities for the national allocation of funds and then because they have this other money, they think let's do something else as well. We have tried to change that. We have said that you must really demonstrate the priority of these projects and we can see that if you devote the part of the national allocation to this as well so we are quite certain that these programs are not simply added on to the national priorities. Obviously the larger the entity, the more difficult it is to manage—i.e., the change in size of the members of the Community. If most of the decisions were taken by means of a majority vote, I think we would probably be completely stymied. So what is possible among six is not possible among 12. If you want to make progress, you must bear this in mind. This obviously means a transfer of part of national sovereignty to the common structure set-up. If you have a large number of members and ECOWAS is a large entity, then you have to be flexible. You should not necessarily want to do everything together. It is quite possible that in a large entity you have variable speed. Within a large entity it is possible to have subgroups that will do certain things together. This is not an option we chose, but the situation evolved naturally. We have the Benelux within the Community and they coexist with the larger group, which is not at the same level of integration. So you can have this type of approach.

My final comment is linked to structural adjustment. If you start to ask to what extent can external partners—the Community, the World Bank, the IMF—support regional groupings, immediately you get into the problems of structural adjustment. Structural adjustment has some positive sides; it is there to facilitate regional cooperation. If we take the example of Ghana, if its economy can adjust and reach rates of exchange that are more realistic, obviously that will be a precondition met for the whole cooperation in that region. So remedying the one country will facilitate trade and cooperation among all the countries in the area. But I would warn you against excessive national approaches to adjustment policy. Here, the World Bank and IMF will have to reconsider their policies. At the moment their approach is too much country based. The policy recommended for the neighboring country is not necessarily compatible with the policy being recommended to the first. If this is the case you can get into extreme situations. Senegal and Gambia— one agricultural policy in the one is completely undermined by the liberalization policy of the neighboring country. As the frontiers are permeable, you cannot protect one policy against the effects of the other. So it is vital for the structural adjustment approach to be compatible within a region, otherwise you might be triggering off erratic and uncontrollable movements given the permeability of these frontiers.

I wonder whether the principle of liberalization of imports should not be considered in the light of regional cooperation because if conditions set by the World Bank or IMF are for liberalization of imports, you have no margin to promote intrazonal liberalization. If you create a customs union, you have to have full freedom within the union, but you have to have some protection outside. One has to consider whether the trade policy recommended to African countries should not be structured so as to favor regional cooperation. This presupposes a level of production outside the regional cooperation entity. If you are thinking about resuscitating regional organizations and want to draw lessons from our own experience (realizing that our experience cannot be fully transferred), we will be at your entire disposal.

Edem Kodjo
Former Secretary General, OAU

It is always good to forecast things, and it is forecasts that are most lacking in Africa. We tend to look at our own small area and immediate needs and forget to look to the future and the problems of the future.

In the ACP dossiers I found very little that could warrant real fears about the 1992 market. When I looked at physical, technical barriers, the problems of services and investment, also current sale monetary matters, I realized that either things were not yet totally clear or that the real risks we are likely

to run in the future are fairly limited. If we look at technical physical barriers, there are a number of products—bananas, rum, textiles, cocoa—but
they should be fairly easily resolved. For cocoa there is the problem of chocolate, but in studying the ACP positions I found that this problem could be
solved by mutual recognition or by enabling African countries producing
other vegetable oils to have access to Community markets. For technical
matters—cadmium in phosphates and the aflatoxin in the ground nuts of
Senegal—the risks are virtually limited to those two. There remains the
multifiber agreement for textiles. We have heard that the MFA will expire
in 1990 and it is by no means certain that it will be renewed in its present
form. As to services, again a lot of fears are expressed, but I have found
from the ACP dossiers that the experts concluded there were not real fears
but a real opportunity for a reduction in interest rates. Therefore this should
lighten some of the debt burden upon us.

On investment, again studying the ACP dossiers, investments made in
Europe are not necessarily the same as the investments that could be made
in Africa. Investors may not just operate on the basis of profit criteria and
the sort of return they are likely to obtain.

On monetary matters, again nothing is very clear because of the franc
zone (CFA). Once the European currency is created, I don't think this will
mean the disintegration of the franc zone. Probably there will have to be
adjustments, perhaps there will be a devaluation of the currencies of the
member countries of the franc zone. But probably because this is politically
desired by the relevant countries, a modus vivendi will be found with a
European currency in the year 2000 and the currencies of the franc zone.
Does this mean that West Africa will continue to be fragmented in monetary
terms? No. I think we need to use this opportunity of monetary negotiation
to bring about the involvement of the other West African countries so that
we can make some progress toward monetary union by encouraging other
countries to have some kind of fixed parity with the ECU. It is a bit of a
paradox that perhaps a monetary union in Africa will be undertaken on the
back of the ECU because European countries feel that there will have to be
a close link between their currency and the ECU, to avoid too many advantages accruing to the countries in the franc zone. So we will get to a
position where the African countries will, because of this European currency, feel themselves interrelated and will be in some kind of a fixed parity
zone. This is what will happen when we have the European currency in the
year 2000. It is not the disintegration of the franc zone and the disunion in
the franc zone. I know that in West Africa and Central Africa, there are
countries that perhaps would no longer exist if the franc zone didn't exist.

These countries would never be convinced to abandon the advantages of the zone in favor of other African units. So we must use that opportunity to undertake global negotiations both between African countries and with the ECU members in order to ensure some kind of stability at the level of our currencies.

The conclusion I reached is that we seem to be speculating about something that doesn't yet exist. We are losing sight of the fact that we are in difficulties now vis-à-vis the present situation. We African countries are in difficulties. For those areas where we have higher comparative costs or lower comparative costs, these opportunities are being wasted. For certain products—palm oil, cocoa, coffee—we did start off with major comparative advantages, and these are being gradually lost, particularly for the palm oil producers. We obviously have to say to Europe, don't become a fortress Europe, don't engage in too much protectionism, but at the same time we have to look to our own house and see what we can do to have satisfactory production costs so that we can remain on the market.

Automatically this leads to ECOWAS because we have to look at the problem from a regional outlook. I can't see a solution by having a restructuring in each of our countries individually organized by the IMF. I think we have to think of restructuring at a regional level so we can see what we can do to bring that about. For us in West Africa, the real challenge we are facing today is what can we do to change ECOWAS. ECOWAS is not working well, the economies of its member states are not complementary, they are dissimilar for all sorts of reasons. But do not think in Europe that there is no problem of competition. Let us look at the ACP and the European markets; there is a great deal of competition. There are a lot of areas where there is stiff competition in Europe; it is by no means certain that all European countries are complementary. Let us not delude ourselves, complementarity is by no means self-evident and the Europeans themselves realize this; this is why they tackle each problem individually. They have made amazing achievements in science and technology. Now they have turned to tax harmonization and harmonization of banking services and are moving on to monetary harmonization. So we should not have too many inhibitions or feel that ECOWAS can't work because our economies are not complementary and because we all produce the same thing. We can render ECOWAS far more dynamic and active. I recommend that we set up an expert group under the leadership of General Obasanjo and look at ECOWAS with a view to resuscitate and revive it. Each country can look at its comparative advantages; we should look at the development plans of each country and from that we should work out a minimal survival plan for ECOWAS. This is something we can do and should tackle. This will lead to lower costs and guarantee productivity. We don't want to come to the Europeans and ask them to help us create ECOWAS; we can do this ourselves. We can do it. Let's take each problem in turn and come up with a survival plan for ECO-WAS. Let us say that these will be the optimal allocations for this industry, for agriculture, for services, and these are the compensations we could give to a given country if a given country was to incur considerable losses.

Louis Emmerij
President, OECD Development Centre

I stand on the delicate bridge between the Organization for Economic Co-operation and Development and the rest of the world. We are discussing the impact of one region on another at a period in time where we see the rise of global markets and global enterprises and simultaneously with the rise of these global markets, the rise of an economic multipolarity, which is ac-companied by the creation of regional economic blocks. But regional eco-nomic blocks do not necessarily introduce protectionism as it is often main-tained but conquer more aggressively and more competitively a bigger component of those global markets. If there is protectionism it is a temporary closing off in order to prepare oneself better. In this world of the 1990s and beyond, we see Africa, not only West Africa, in a very difficult situation. Africa is on the slow track of world economic development, and not only on the slow track but a track that may be going in a different direction as compared to the main thrust of world economic development. The World Bank and UNDP have issued a report showing that African economies are doing better than one often says. It is important psychologically not to talk all the time about doom and pessimism, so I appreciate this report. But we should not delude ourselves. Africa is in a difficult situation and it is almost being delinked involuntarily from the main thrust of world development.

There are advantages and disadvantages for Africa to be on that slow and quasi-delinked track. The advantage is that it gives one time to sit back and reflect and do something about development strategies. It is true, Africa may have been too influenced by the rest of the world in designing its economic and social development policies, so a period of introspection may be useful in this slow track situation and not being a member really of an existing economic block. I come to the conclusion that a period of introspection and redesigning of economic policies, more appropriate to the African situation, is the crucial problem. It is not 1992, it is diversifying African economies. Those economies have been much too static. The world has been moving fast and Africa is staying as it was. There is something beautiful in staying as one was, but not in a global market and a competitive situation. African nations must use this period to design a strategy that diversifies their economies, that makes them more competitive in order to join not only Europe 1992 but the global market. For that, they must also take regional integration much more seriously. They must become a block in their own right, not to be delinked, not to shut themselves off but to open up in a more competitive way to open up the global market.

Gary Busch
Chairman and Managing Director, Tetraview Ltd., London

As a non-European and a non-African, I have perhaps a different view. It occurred to me that one of the great problems is: what is it we are talking about in Europe? What is the engine of European integration? The engine of European integration is the European companies. It is not the European governments, it is the European companies. 1992 is already here. GEC plus Siemens were talking about setting up mega-European corporations, making Europe safe for the junk bond salesman. This means, as is clear from the statements made by the various parts of the EEC Commission, that they are looking for developing a large rationalized European market. This means that instead of producing a variety of goods within the European communities, they are going to horizontally integrate this type of production throughout Europe. So, instead of producing in Germany, they will be able to move to Greece to take advantage of the particular Greek situation, they will be able to move to Spain and Portugal to take advantage of those. This is where the direct investments are going to be going. This is the type of investment of unifying a large multinational or transnational European corporation. It seems that between now and 1992 the European Commission can act as a brake or an accelerator, but it does not have the steering wheel or the engine.

Now the problem with trying to deal with it from Africa is: what is Africa going to sell, to what market is it going to sell it, and who is going to give the investment to allow the African countries to compete with the type of economic investments that will be taking place throughout the least advantaged areas in Europe? I don't have the solution, but until there is an integrated market where Africans can sell to other Africans and where there is trade in commodities from one African country to another, there will be no engine in Africa for the governments to regulate. There is no movement internally; it is a response not a forward direction. This is very serious. The Europe that exists today is not a Europe of free competition, it is a large group of semicartels or official cartels that deal within the European Communities. Which is, of course, being regulated by the EEC and they are trying to control it, but it is no mystery that if you want to buy types of steel, there is a steel cartel, likewise for coal, etc. If you want to buy various building products, there are unofficial price arrangements, which are the rule and not the exception. Of course, the competition policies attempt to regulate it, but they are usually a few steps behind. The governments themselves cannot control it and certainly an organization of governments' government can't control it.

What is left is what price will they pay for African products and are they going to pay for primary products, because primary products are needed to fuel the European integration. So I would suspect that if we are going to address the problem of the impact of the EEC in 1992 on Africa, that should be one of the key areas.

Patrick Agboh
Secretariat, ACP, Brussels

References have been made to what the ACP Secretariat can do to help the process of development in West Africa. We have considered the subject matter of regional cooperation and a single market before deciding on our strategy for the ongoing negotiations. At the outset, we considered the international developments taking place, including the single market, the Uruguay round, the Common Agricultural policy, and the general situation in commodity markets. Then we arrived at the central objective of the ACP, which was that we have to try as much as possible to get the capacity to diversify our economies away from extreme dependence on raw material exports into the processing field, processing not only for domestic markets, which has to be expanded, but also for exports. Therefore, the trade arrangements have to be strengthened and improved. We have to improve the access of our products and wherever possible preserve the preferences that we enjoy. We had difficulties over this. First, the Uruguay round is ensuring that much of the preferences and also the GSP have actually contributed to the erosion of the preferences. We also asked for the liberalization of the rules of origin, as they act as a major disincentive to investment in our countries. We had some difficulty in getting our partners to agree to this kind of position.

Having decided on the need for restructuring of our economies, we also realized that many of our countries are very small, most of them, about 20, with a population of less than one million people. Because we want to be able to pool our resources and achieve economies of scale, regional cooperation is one of the major objectives we have selected. The experience we have gained so far has made it very difficult to be optimistic, but there are certain positive sides we have seen in other parts of Africa, particularly from southern Africa and the PTA region.

We also have to review what is happening to our approach in West Africa in particular. In some cases, especially in Europe, we find that it is the private sector that is pushing the integration process much more in Europe. Through research, companies are able to find the benefits they expect from these projects and so the integration is not being promoted so much by government but by the private companies. The other issue with regional cooperation is the question of payment facilities for trade, which has been one of the impediments. This is one key subject that we will be discussing intensely with the partners.

Human resources are the key; humans being the agent of development are at the same time beneficiaries. All questions about the effects of structural adjustment on the human condition is therefore being taken very seriously. What we expect from our Community partners is not to make it difficult for our nationals to enter these countries and move freely, to pursue their vocations or studies without any hindrance. They must move freely so that greater cultural interaction can benefit our countries.

The process of European integration has been going on for some time but it is only now that we are trying to react. This is why it is important to consider all aspects of our relationship in a multi-sectoral way in order to give specific attention to the productive sectors, agriculture, industry and particularly transportation. The movement of companies in Europe towards mega-companies will have an effect on our productive units that can only be guessed. We must also focus on investment flows into our countries, as some will find that investment in Europe is more attractive than investment in Africa. In the next Lomé convention provisions must be included to foster aid flows into our countries. In the present negotiations, proposals have been made by ACP for special facilities to guarantee aid flows and for facilities to assist small investors. But this is not finding the support we expected from our partners. There is a tendency that aid flows are falling and something has to be done about this. If this is now being tied to structural adjustment, the effect can be quite dangerous in the future.

As regards technical barriers, we have seen that certain duties had to be withdrawn because their effect was inimical to our development. Our only hope in the future is to ensure that the consultation procedures are strengthened. Everybody has to try as much as possible to consult in earnest and be bound by the position of the two parties.

I have doubts about the pool effect of growth in Europe on development in West African countries. Whenever there was considerable recovery in Europe in past years, we have seen a downward trend in Africa. Where a weak country finds itself in association with a strong country, the weak get weaker and the strong get stronger unless special measures are taken. Growth in consumer goods demand will only benefit countries who have already started on the road and who are in a stronger position than countries in West Africa. There is also a question of our economic structures which are weak and unable to respond quickly to changing situations somewhere in Europe. How can our countries begin or expect to compete with a country like South Korea? All this points to the need on the part of our partners to provide whatever kind of assistance they can in the form of trade promotion.

Gerald Blakey
Adviser, West Africa Committee, London

It may be helpful to make some remarks from the private sector. The views I express are those of the members of the organizations that are members of the West Africa Committee. The organization I represent has probably 1,500–1,600 members who are major investors in Africa. The West Africa Committee has 130. These are banks, oil companies, construction companies. Perhaps more importantly, I can speak for other associations such as the Africa Institute from the Netherlands, the Afrika-Verein from Germany, CCPA from Brussels, SIAN from France, a new member from Portugal ELO, and soon to join we hope a corresponding organization from Spain. This organization is collectively and rather confusingly known as the Group of 7 investors in ACP countries, unrelated to the G-7 group of industrialized countries.

One way of approaching the private sector view is a look at what investors require when they place their money offshore. There are five factors that the potential investor is going to look at before he puts his hand in his pocket. These are: viability, commitment, investment protection, control, and remission. I will run through those against the context of investment in Africa and against the background of what has been said about the developments of 1992 and how it will affect them.

First, viability. The first thing that any investor wants is a fair return. There is no doubt that there have been offshore investors in Africa who have tried to take much more than a fair return. The membership of my organizations is looking for a fair return on investment. Then what is the competition as far as placing this money is concerned? I suggest that it is intense. There are a large number of investment opportunities that are becoming more and more attractive, and perhaps internal investment in Europe is one of these. There are also the Far Eastern organizations—the Singapore Development Corporation, interesting developments in China, the opening up of the Communist block. But Africa, and it is perhaps easier to talk about sub-Saharan Africa generally although all that I say applies to West Africa, has many attractions, not the least of which is its market size. It is an enormous market in terms of population. But, of course, a market full of people with no money in their pockets is not necessarily a good market to do business in. Nevertheless, even the scale of the potential size of the African market is such that if you make biros and you can sell a biro to one in four people in a country the size of Nigeria, you are in a big business. And, of course,

West Africa has natural resources. So the first criteria is: is it viable or would I be better off putting my money in the bank down the road?

The second point is commitment. The first subfactor must be political will. Is there the political support from the countries in Africa to accept investment? Superficially, it appears that there may be. There are statements on industrial policy, investment policy, but I suspect that there is still a certain subconscious reluctance to accept offshore money and the historic reasons and some current evidence are clear. But this must be overcome, there must be a real political will. It is something that we in the UK have found difficult to accept. I find that Coopers Old English Marmelade is actually owned by the Kellogg Company in Texas. You have to accept that it is a fact of international trade that offshore money will penetrate what have seemed to be important parts of your economy. Also there are certain sectors—energy resources and defense—that understandably must be fully protected. Then there must be real local enthusiasm for working together. There is particularly good cooperation between the Europeans and the Africans on working for joint ventures on back-to-back operations. Then there is local participation—there are 1.3 million Nigerian investors in the Nigerian stock exchange who collectively put in one-half a billion U.S. dollars into the Nigerian economy. It is not widely known, but that sort of local enthusiasm is going to be an important factor in the decision of the offshore investor as to whether to become involved. Although I am disappointed to hear that the ACP initiative on small businesses is not being widely supported, their expansion in Europe is significant in the context of a comparable expansion in Africa. I think particularly of Ghana, where a special secretariat has been set up to help and encourage this.

The third point that the potential investor is looking for is investment protection. We have already touched on the importance of political stability. There is nothing more discouraging than picking up your paper and finding that there has been a major coup in a country where you have a major investment. Investors are looking for government assurances both from their own governments and from governments of the countries in which they invest. Progress is being made in investment protection and agreements. A series of such agreements were recently signed between a number of European countries and Ghana. The question of investment protection also touches on export credit guarantees. Perhaps there is an opportunity for a coordinated European initiative. Already, the various national export guarantee agencies do work together unofficially. Maybe this should be coordinated to produce a better service for the offshore investor. There has been an interesting development as far as the World Bank is concerned with MIGA, the multinational investment guarantee agency, but it is a little underfunded and quite expensive in market terms. So, there is an opportunity for a European initiative here.

Fourth, the investor is looking for control of his investment. Some of the policies extended from African countries say "send a cheque but don't come yourself!" The question of quotas and the question of an equity participation are very important indeed. Again, I think there is an historical reluctance to accept that you may need experts in order to ensure that an investment is profitable. But there is no reason to be shy about accepting experts. For example, in the UK when our steel industry was in disarray, we turned to the United States and we hired the best steel man in the world to turn it around, which he did. I believe that you should hire the expertise to work for you, in some of these areas, particularly the higher technological areas. The same goes for equity participation. There is considerable apprehension about putting a stake into an organization if you don't have a reasonable amount of control over it.

Assuming that the previous four criteria are met, that the money is there and is working, there is the question of remission. Offshore investors invest so that their investment will come home to roost. The question of taxation, the disincentives of excess profits' tax, withholding tax, etc. are very important to the offshore investor. But the most important factor is the question of exchange risk. Many have had successful business years in 1988–89, have perhaps made 25 percent profits, which they would consider a fair return. But when they attempt to remit that money, the exchange rate is such that they end up with a net loss. The implications of financial stability, this is going to be an essential factor if offshore money is going to come confidently into West Africa. The CFA zone has worked, albeit with considerable difficulties. The sterling zone in a previous era worked reasonably well. I believe that Europe perhaps as much as an aid measure as a commercial measure should make a very determined effort to try and introduce that sort of financial stability.

To end perhaps on a philosophical note, I believe that the one objective of this conference on West Africa should be to try and accentuate the special relationship that must exist between Europe and Africa. Our historical ties, the geographic closeness, the fact that we are on the same time zone, our languages, our familiarity with contract procedures, and the fact that we know each other and are friends. As friends we can talk frankly to each other, we can disagree, we can have major rows on occasion. It is very important. Just as Japan is developing a relationship with Southeast Asia, that the United States has developed a relationship with South America, I believe that the ties between Europe and Africa should be developed in a very special way.

On Infrastructure Requirements

To comment on the infrastructure requirements of offshore investors is quite demanding because different sectors and different scales of industry have different requirements. The multinationals can really move into a green field or desert site with no infrastructure requirements. They have the financial backing and can look far enough ahead to do what is required to run their business, e.g., the hugely successful cement works at El Sharka, which you see as a dot on the desert horizon. In contrast, the SMEs (small and medium businesses) require much more. What is needed to help both here and in Europe? I think back to the Welsh Development Board and what they offer to attract people, also to the same sort of opportunities offered in some West African countries: basic requirements of having access to a commercial site, to having water there, and to have a reliable source of electricity. You can then arrive, set up your business, and go into production. Those are the basics.

Beyond that there is a requirement for a number of facilities that the offshore investor probably takes for granted elsewhere. You must be able to communicate (in the general sense) not only to get on the telephone, telex, fax, but the overall transportation infrastructure, airports, reasonable facilities for moving in and out, roads, etc. The question of human resources is very important. There must be some midlevel management support. Perhaps there are opportunities for mutual aid in that area. Also important is a reliable labor force. Hopefully, the investor will have the opportunity to draw on some marketing organizations, perhaps local consultancies and all the service organizations essential to manufacturing and investment. Finally, the question of physical security is very important. The businessman must feel that he is going to be safe and he is able to operate in a reasonable environment.

Emile van Lennep
former Secretary General, OECD

I was present and actively participated in the negotiations that created the Common Market in the 1950s. I have therefore clearly seen what the motivations at that time were and what the problems were. It is always essential to keep well in mind what really economic integration is and what it means. It does aim at more welfare, more growth through more trade, which opens up trade for a more competitive producer, which has the direct impact of lower prices and more competitivity for the area as a whole. It is good to keep this in mind because it can be done by trade creation and by trade diversion. If opening up trade within the area goes at a cost of competitive producers outside, increases or keeps high import duties for the outside world, then, of course, it leads to trade diversion. If, in contrast, it keeps open markets, then the lower prices and the more competitivity will lead to more trade and also not just either trade diversion or trade creation. But if it is trade creation, then it is trade expansion. The lower prices lead to higher demand within and also to the outside world not just for commodities but generally.

A view of 1992 will lead and should lead with appropriate external policies to higher growth and generally higher demand also for products from Africa of various sorts (tourism, manufactured goods, commodities). It is good to keep in mind that such welfare gains are obtained the more the structures of the economies are similar and the more the production costs are divergent. This is shown very clearly by economic theory. It is not true that economic integration is a good thing if you have complementary economies; on the contrary, economic integration really creates welfare gains if the structures are similar because then within the area you have the more productive, more competitive producer who gains the market at the cost of the less competitive producer in the area. It is appropriate to remind oneself about this if we talk about the impact of 1992 on Africa.

It has been said, and I share this view, that the problem is not just 1992, the problem is access to the markets now and in the future in a global economy. The excess will be gained by the more competitive producer. The EEC producers as a group will become more competitive as a consequence of completing economic integration and therefore all producers outside the EEC have to look at whether they are competitive in this European market as we should be in general, because it might become more difficult in Europe. The same goes for Africa. It has been said that Africa is somewhat lagging behind, that their competitive position is inadequate and therefore it is very important to think very hard how one can improve one's competitive position. Not just by thinking in monetary terms of devaluation but by really getting the more competitive producers to come ahead and to come to life.

A regional approach within a global market has shown to be effective, a regional approach that is open to the rest of the world; otherwise the welfare gains will not be made. A regional approach is an effective approach to promote competition and lower prices.

I support fully what Edem Kodjo said earlier. I think that the follow-up of this important meeting should be to think hard about that approach and not just having another report that economic integration is a good thing. How can one make practical steps forward? There one should realize that the economic integration process is always a process of accepting costs to obtain benefits in the future. One should accept the costs of the inefficient producers who lose market shares for the benefit of the efficient producers. These are visible costs for individual firms, and although I fully share the view that the private sector should be the engine of economic growth and also of integration, it is those firms who fear that they will be excluded who will go to the governments and say that I will be the victim, you must help me. This happened in Europe in the 1950s, and immediately there were plans for big adaptation fund to compensate for these losses, which were inevitable.

I would recommend the following: start an integration process step by step with small concrete steps and not be tempted by long discussions about compensations of costs where the whole machinery might be created that transfers funds from here to there. First of all, it is impossible to identify who these losers are and second, it leads to a big machinery that only diverts the attention from the enormous benefits aimed at to individual noncompetitive firms. When I talked with Jean Monet about why European supranational integration started with coal and steel, I said that as an economist there is no rationale to start in one sector. The integration is a process for the economy as a whole. He said it is quite clear, it is not logic. I agree, but it was the only real, practical political step. It was clear to everybody that it was needed and possible in economic terms. That is the only justification; it is a limited step that will have its follow-up later. It did. Gradually all these vertical integration plans were succeeded by the general customs union and European integration. I would suggest the same approach for Africa. Look at practical limited steps to start with. Don't talk about the cost. Talk about the efficiency and urgency of the problem of getting competitive.

When we started our difficult negotiations in the 1950s, we had indeed the benefit of the political will and effective leadership in the negotiations. West Africa needs both of these things. The political will means to be convinced of the need to do so. There is an urgent need to start this process as soon as possible. West Africa needs a leader to start negotiating and getting things done.

Kandeh Yilla
General Secretary, Sierra Leone Labour Congress

By background, I am a trade unionist. Being from a developing situation, we are concerned with the Lomé Conventions and we are getting ourselves ready for the ongoing discussions of Lomé IV. The effective participation of trade unions hinges sometimes on repressive measures in some of our countries. Trade unionists have always been on the verge of being thrown into the cemeteries to the extent that we are not taken so much into consideration when talking about matters that affect development as a whole.

In our discussions, we were able to come up with wide-ranging recommendations that we hope could be channelled through the various authorities (governments, international trade union associations) before the final text of Lomé IV is completed. Some of these include respect for human and trade union rights, which we cannot divorce from human rights, and these are most often abused. They also include a means of lightening the economic difficulties of debt-laden countries and also measures to guarantee the rights of eight ACP member countries within the EEC when the internal market is finally realized.

Structural or recovery programs in our part of the world will continue to fail because they are not normally based on a high degree of consensus, both in terms of objectives and efforts. There has been reference to the creation of structures. Unless and until our governments recognize that economic development and growth are directly linked to the creation of democratic structures, we will definitely fail. This position has to be revised. When I talk about democratic structures, I mean trade unions whose leaderships are not imposed by political leaders and, of course, other partners. Sometimes our institutions in Africa tend to fail because of some similar reasons. The political will may be there, but what sort of education? The appropriate education relevant to our society and circumstances is sometimes lacking. Taking into consideration the political will to create ECOWAS without the mobilization of the masses to give that added support for it to succeed, I am afraid we will be wasting our time.

———— ◆•◆ ————

Victor Mpoyo
Industrialist

The real issue, at the heart of this forum, is the training of our future leaders, of young people who have to take over from us and consolidate the regional economic units we wish to set up. The private sector can propose greater relations with the assistance of the Community so that we can receive teachers/trainers in our own countries to organize the training of our young managers in the private sector, so that these managers in turn can assist the economic agents to organize themselves better. Hitherto we have talked about the market. In Europe there is a reorganization and consolidation underway of their market. We do not have consumers for the products that we have been considering. So how can we consolidate if we do not have consumption, domestic demand? We are still asking for aid assistance and foreign loans. But I think the most important problem is to create a market of domestic consumers. Once we have encouraged our people to consume, it will encourage the economic agents to produce for them. Until such time as we have consumers in our own countries, how do you expect the development to move away from exports? At the moment we are developing only to export—to supply raw materials, semifinished products to industries located elsewhere.

———— ◆•◆ ————

Isaac Akinrele

Director, Centre for the Development of Industry, Brussels

The desire to set up a single market in Europe has been stimulated by an economic necessity to compete in a global environment dominated by high technology and advanced corporate management. If that, in fact, is the thrust given to the single-market approach then it cannot really bend backward to dilute the conditions necessary to be competitive. Of course, it is not exactly the same thing as aid. The aid policy is not within the context of a single market. It might have some effect on it, but it is not a major consideration in bringing about the objectives of a single market for the Community. I have no doubt that it is an objective that will be achieved. I think the objectives will be achieved because there are instruments that are being set up to make them achievable. There is a legislative framework in the context of the European Parliament; you have the Treaty of Rome; the European Commission is working for this objective; you have a fiscal policy that controls access to the European market; you have a financial instrument in terms of the European Investment Bank; you have the political and international clout of the Community, which is always expressed in the Bretton Woods institutions—the OECD, the Paris and London clubs. These are major instruments that influence world trade and therefore the Community.

Another aspect that is not very much publicized is the rejection and deployment of uncompetitive and unviable investments. This could be a politically sensitive thing as many people could be displaced or investments could be displaced as a result of the higher competition brought about by the single market. Of course, one must also look at the access to the market. Europe cannot afford to establish a fortress. It has to trade with the rest of the world, and therefore it will only liberalize its market on the basis of reciprocity. If the ground rules were to be accepted but while advocating to reach other markets through better competition, it would in fact open its own market; then those that can benefit from such access will be those that can compete. Competition means that you can supply a product with clear comparative and competitive advantages.

In contrast, when you look at the ECOWAS region, which would be a natural counterpart to the Community, it is not a trading partner to the Community. Its individual member states trade with Europe. There is no infrastructure to discuss trade between ECOWAS and the Community. There is the Lomé Convention of which ECOWAS is a member, not as ECOWAS but as individual members. ECOWAS has set up a number of protocols; there is an institutional framework for meetings and taking positions, but really it does not have economic clout. Neither does it have the capacity to negotiate any special arrangements for West Africa. ECOWAS as a group does not even have the framework to negotiate special arrangements. The economic base of ECOWAS is really that as a commodity supplier and it does not supply directly to the consumer; it supplies via intermediaries who are private commercial institutions. So when the value of its commodity earnings declines, it is sometimes difficult to know whether the declining earnings are determined by free market pricing or through manipulations of intermediaries. Given this situation, the immediate priority for ECOWAS in responding to the market that might be unified in Europe is to attempt to organize structures so that it can produce a competitive framework. It should look for and try to plan for value-added production, raw materials of better quality so that it can compete with other regions of the world such as Southeast Asia. I think it is not just a matter of price negotiation, it is in fact improving the production structure to enable African nations to use their comparative advantage and transfer it into a competitive advantage.

What will fall out from the single market in Europe? There will have to be a massive investment, redeployment of the SMEs. Many of the SMEs in the Community will not survive likely because of higher competition and stricter standards. They will move as well. This is where West Africa could offer an attractive alternative. Some will want to retain their market share of West Africa and they will now find a comparative advantage in relocating there. In some cases relocating can even become competitive in order to re-enter the Common Market. Then there will be an opportunity for commodity processing because the market in Europe, which will become highly competitive, will be looking for raw materials, semiprocessed materials for these industries in order to have the competitive edge. It might be an opportunity to arrange subcontracting production for major multinational production or treatment of processing of commodity products if a suitable investment framework could be worked out. We are involved on a day-to-day basis to try to identify investors, industrialists in developing investment, and industrial cooperation with entrepreneurs in Africa and the Caribbean and the Pacific. We see a considerable interest in this. To be able to assure that profit is made not only financially but also in social terms, there is a need to assist cooperation enterprises of this nature by carefully negotiating the framework of production for a joint investment. I think it would be a very useful thing if the ECOWAS secretariat can get interested in the possibility of assisting the member states of West Africa to create a framework for joint ventures and investment with industrialists from Europe. It must also be mentioned that to be very pragmatic, we would be deluding ourselves if we think that an enterprise in an environment that is handicapped can ever be competitive. In fact the idea of providing leverage for areas that are handicapped is practiced in the Community. You have special areas assisted with special development funds, etc. I think both West Africa and the European Community should look at the concessionality that can be given to absorb the handicap involved in the infrastructures of the West African countries and to be able to produce competitively for the domestic and Community market. I think it is from this perspective that the Lomé Convention can go a long way to give assurance to the long-standing relationship between the Community and the ACP states.

Richard C. Greenhalgh
Senior Member, Africa and Middle East Regional Management,
Unilever, London

Unilever operates in 15 African countries, and in seven of them we are in manufacturing. 1992 is in a way a catalyst, not a trigger, for what is going on in the world. We have this rapid globalization of many of our industries. We have the searching with ever-increasing speed for international brands, and we have the concentration on regional markets. Multinationals are particularly focusing on the triad of United States, Europe, and Japan. There are mergers going on. Large mergers such as Plessey/GEC in Europe and elsewhere. All this will lead to a tremendous reorganization in Europe around 1992.

If you look at my own business, we have 100 manufacturing plants around Europe. It has already been stated in the press that we will have considerably fewer in the 1990s. There will be a concentration of many competitive multinationals in Europe and that has risks for Africa. Why? Investment could well be put into Europe rather than into Africa. We know that private investment levels in Africa are already low, but anything that moves in the wrong direction we can only be concerned about.

Second, in the area of people there is a risk. We as multinationals are concerned to develop Africans in Europe and to send Europeans into Africa. I think there may be some difficulties in the next few years in terms of the concentration on creating genuine European managers rather than Dutch managers, German managers, French managers, or British managers. Again, it is a question of emphasis that there may well be concentration on Europe to the detriment of Africa.

The third concern I have about this rationalization in Europe is in the area of product development. Product development will be focused on these international brands, some of which, of course, are relevant to Africa, but it may again tilt against Africa's interests.

Through the eyes of the African consumer, we see a market where the growth of the population is higher than the growth of the economies and there is a considerable amount of down trading in the products that are being purchased. One example of that is in soaps and detergents. If you go back 10 years, my company and our competitors thought that the African market would be moving fast toward detergent powders; in fact, it is now going back toward hard soaps and the use of hard soap for washing clothes, etc. We can't counteract that market; that is what the consumer wants. What we would like to do as a company is have the development to make even better hard soaps than we can at the moment. Better in terms of what the consumer wants. But we need economies of scale for that to tailor those products for Africa. Hence the comments we have had about regionalism and ECOWAS and the PTA in East Africa. I can only emphasize the advantages if that could genuinely happen. We have talked a lot about exporting from Africa, and rightly so, but there is also importing from Africa. I have spoken to a number of exporters from Europe exporting into Africa and there is concern that as we get ever larger plants in Europe, will there be the right products to export to Africa? A number of companies are now looking at Asia as a source of products for Africa. Asia is already a large exporter into Africa.

I can only underline Gerald Blakey's remarks made earlier about the climate for inward investment. I think the climate is infinitely better than it was five years ago. Take the case of Ghana, which has dramatically turned around in five years. Also, to create the right climate for reinvestment, reinvestment is the right support to agriculture to improve yields, in the areas of seed multiplication, for example. I would also suggest that the right climate for people to come and work there is important. The number of expatriates is declining which is good, but there will be a requirement still for expatriates in Africa. If we can get easier quota situations and remittance situations, then the right quality of expatriate can be encouraged to enter Africa.

Finally, two examples on regionalism. The most successful West African regional trading zone is in the area of African prints and textiles. They move freely along trading paths with no boundaries. They move by smugglers. They move from country to country. If the smugglers can do it, so can governments. Second, cooperation between African countries. I was privileged to attend the opening of the edible oil plant. It was a large investment, it created employment, and has African managers. The only thing is that the large majority of raw material is palm oil imported from Malaysia. If we could have this from other African countries, it would be better. The concentration on regional trading links must be right.

Alassane F. Ouattara
Governor, Banque Centrale des Etats de l'Afrique de l'Ouest

I don't see divergences or insurmountable problems or any embarrassing uncertainty. I think a reinforced stronger Common Market is a good thing for Africa. It will mean greater opportunity, a larger trade area, and this opens up new perspectives. If countries are small and the area is small, any broader larger association gives at least broader openings. As Europe is strengthened, we should strengthen our cooperation.

Let me comment on the monetary cooperation aspects. I don't see any uncertainty and I am rather surprised that there should be the possibility of a revision. Obviously we must always be prepared to think about the future and prepare ourselves, but those of us who are familiar with the mechanisms of the franc zone will understand that even a monetary Europe with a single central bank will not pose any danger for the franc zone and for the West African monetary union in particular.

Carol Lancaster (chapter 3) and Ken Dadzie (this chapter) said that monetary union could be an obstacle to greater integration within ECOWAS. I am rather surprised at that because convertibility is vital for economic growth and perhaps indeed for the well-being of the area. I don't think there is one country in the subarea where the CFA franc is not used as a national currency. So, on the contrary, we are seventh, and an eighth country has applied to join and we may add one or two other members in the next few years. Any monetary policy must be seen in the context of the macro-economic framework. Integration is vital. It is something we must all pursue.

But we also need individuality to set order in our own houses. It is not just by getting together that we can solve all problems from outside. A stable currency, not necessarily strong but one that is appropriate for the economic circumstances of a country is vital for economic integration. So, I would be delighted if convertibility could be extended and if the national currencies in the other countries in our region could be acceptable throughout the region as that would show that monetary policy is compatible.

To turn to exchange rates and devaluation. We have to be very careful. European monetary union, whatever the consequences for Europe, does not necessarily mean a devaluation of the CFA franc. We have to look at the CFA franc in relation to our own policies and above all as a result of measures that we will implement to control costs. I am delighted that a country such as Senegal had a negative rate of inflation last year. That might not lead to long-term growth, but nevertheless Senegal had a growth rate of 5 percent with negative inflation. I think if we compare the rate of exchange of the CFA and the rate of exchange in the parallel markets in neighboring countries, it is not the CFA franc that is overvalued, it is the other currencies if you look at the official exchange rates.

To sum up, there is no uncertainty either on monetary union or on exchange rates, or about our desire for a broader monetary policy, and I think there should be no fears about parities of exchange rates. So what should we do to weld ourselves closer together? I think this is something that can only be looked at in the long term. We have to think together. I would entirely agree with Edem Kodjo that we should embark on practical specific steps. We have to carry out structural reform, not of the infrastructure or of tangible matters but in a mental sense. Economic integration can only start with very specific things, just as the coal and steel community. In the subregion we must be able to meet together and engage in something practical. It is fine to have institutions, but I think it would be better if each of us could think of things that could weld us closer together. If we look at the four major countries of ECOWAS—Cote d'Ivoire, Nigeria, Senegal, and Ghana—I am rather optimistic because the economic policies in those countries are better than they were 10 years ago. Structural measures are in force and despite the difficulties of the external economy, these countries are persisting with their efforts. I think the international economy must help us to grow better. Growth also means competitiveness. We can promote competitively via devaluation, but I don't really believe in that unless there is also a problem of internal demand. Diversification can also be found by adopting structural measures. I think we have to pursue this course in the four countries concerned. I think there is a diversification potential. To remain competitive, a number of countries whose currency is totally under-valued, such as some countries in Southeast Asia, should be encouraged by the European Community to have more appropriate rates of exchange. If they had real rates of exchange reflecting their real situation, we would not be in the situation of surplus production of cocoa, palm oil, or any other products. They have costs that do not reflect the external realities. In my own country, Cote d'Ivoire, we have always had a surplus on the trade balance. In 1988 despite the economic crisis, surplus on the trade balance was $1,000 million. Exports are $2.5 billion, imports are $1.5 billion. So this area has a potential. We must be better organized and above all have follow-up.

———————————— ◆•◆ ————————————

Mamoudou Touré
Director, African Department, IMF

The title of this conference is both a limited and vast topic. Africa is on a siding at the moment. It seems to be locked up until the year 2000. It is up to Africa to get out of this siding. I wish to stress this but I don't wish to dwell on it as it is being dealt with in other forms. If we were to look at the consequences of 1992 on Africa, I think that there are a number of areas that could come into question: the elimination of physical barriers, technical barriers, harmonization of taxation, but in all of these areas we can only assess the effects on Africa once the decisions have been taken under each of these headings. There are economic policy options that will have to be adopted. For each of these headings and without knowledge, I think it is only speculation. Nonetheless there is a general approach that could be in-ferred not just from the past but also by projecting into the future because after all the efforts to bring about European integration are not just recent.

The Community started in 1958 and at the time I was a French official seconded to the European Community from 1958 to 1961. Effects took place then on Africa and I think we can anticipate the effects of closer integration on African countries. I don't really want to dwell on these points, but I would like to stress that we are entering into a world where, despite one's historical ties and feelings of closeness, what really governs our relationships are our relative interests. You like Africa, but if Africa didn't give you anything, you would drop it. Blunt, but I think that is the case. So to promote the blossoming of feeling and emotional ties and to turn these emotional ties into realities, we have to safeguard the various interests. The level of trade, I think everyone knows what is likely to happen. But on investment, I would like to comment. Clearly, public aid for development, even if it is improving in sub-Saharan Africa because of the intolerable pictures we see on TV of young children dying of hunger, cannot continue indefinitely. So we have to have a process of replacement of private investment. This must be generated by creating the appropriate conditions in Africa itself. We must realize that it is no longer possible to rely on public aid for the development of Africa. We have to rely on private investment as well, both national and foreign investment. When I say national investment, don't be surprised. We do have savings in Africa despite the prevailing conditions, but these savings tend to go abroad. Therefore the economic conditions in Africa must be such as to attract both national savings and foreign savings. Financing national investment. We can be helped with the transfer of technology, and I think we have to leave to one side our national pride to some extent to try and promote investment that is, if possible, not generating debt. I mean by this that foreigners are prepared to run risks in our countries and they must therefore be given conditions that are conducive to investment. I think our generation will have to tackle matters of this nature and not desperately stick to national pride. A country in debt does not have any national pride. So if there is a lesson we can draw from the economic integration of Europe, it is that today we have talked about African integration more than anything else. Now, if we have again been obliged to look at the ways in which we can promote integration in Africa, it is because of the example of European integration. It is on the basis of what we have seen achieved in Europe and the challenge that that represents.

The first consequence is that it will probably promote the development of integration in Africa. In 1958 there were very few African countries that were independent. I think it is indispensable to develop the African economy, but integration must also mean being open to the outside because an integrated African market will have and must have as a potential market outlet the whole world. There is no reason why Africa should remain in misery and in the depths of underdevelopment while other countries that were miserable 20 years ago are now highly industrialized. Why should Africa not be capable of doing that? This is something we can do but, we have to abandon the facile approach and don't pay heed to the siren call of external constraints. If we are united none will be able to impose things on us that are counter to our interests. So it is there that we have to seek a solution.

I would like to express a wish, or perhaps more of a prayer. Nowadays, frontiers no longer make economic sense. Japanese and European firms set up in the United States to produce for the American market, American firms set up in South Korea, Taiwan, etc. to produce for those markets and the United States market. Nothing should prevent Europe or Africa from developing, on the basis of what we have already, similar relations if we can restore trust on both sides. This trust should not be based on emotional ties but on reciprocal interests. More than trust we need an act of faith, faith on the part of the Community that Africa has the potential to move out of being permanently assisted and become an equal trading partner. But a faith also on the part of Africa that the foreign partner has an important role to play in the development process, and that that partner must find advantages and stable and appealing conditions. It is these conditions that will attract new investors to Africa. Therefore the internal market, instead of becoming a closing up that would be damaging to Africa and to the long-term interests of Europe and incompatible with the world role of the Community, should lead to promoting cooperation between a better structured Europe and the economies in Africa, which are in great transformation. Rather than speculate on disintegration in Africa, I want to stick to reality and be African from my head to my toes.

So the countries of West Africa must take steps to put order in our own houses, attract investment, and reinforce our cohesion. The integration of the Community will represent a watershed. The impact on other regions in the world will probably be considerable. There is still a great deal to be done in West Africa to strengthen cooperation between the member states. The EEC could help the countries of West Africa to strengthen their integration, particularly by financing a larger part of the projects of a regional nature and also by granting technical assistance to institutions of the union. It is clear that it is in the interests of Europe for its African partners to be organized in viable regional units, thereby offering better conditions for cooperation. Consequently the achievement of 1992 in Europe will make it clear to government and business people in Africa that viable economic units are the solution of the future. To sum up, the idea of economic and social development—the dice have been thrown by Europe—but these dice will be taken up by resolute people, will there not be Africans among them?

Adamu Ciroma

former Governor, Central Bank of Nigeria and former Minister for Industries and Finance

The development in Europe is in a way no more than Europeans changing from trying to protect their interests to promoting their interests. African response should be very positive. A negative response does not deal with the problems they may cause or the opportunities thay may offer. We have no option but at the least to protect our interests and we should really try to go a little further and promote our interests.

Whatever body is available, we should set up to listen and to study what the Europeans are doing so that appropriate response and steps could be taken to collaborate with them, to protect our interests, and to maximize and promote these interests. These responses can be made singly but preferably collectively as there is already a framework, ECOWAS, and other units designed to bring about unity or regional groupings on the African continent. The main problem is not access to the market, because as producers of primary products so far we are natural allies to the development in Europe. They welcome us just as indeed we should find it easy to deal with them as primary producers. It is when you look beyond that that the problems begin. It is necessary not only to consider our positions as primary producers but to look ahead at the possibilities of being something else. The issue is not the details such as prices of bananas, etc. The fact is that Africa is producing many other products that are being sold to Europe as primary products. Some of these products have disappeared. They are no longer being produced in surplus because the prices became so low that the producers abandoned production. The question of price assumes great importance. Whereas other products receive fair prices, the prices of produce from Africa have actually fallen below what they were 20 or 30 years ago.

Is it an accident that there is an debt overhang? It is not immediately part of this problem, but they are related. There was a time when it was possible for Africa and other developing countries to contract so many loans that it is beyond their capacity to repay. The factor of interest is becoming part of the process that has reversed the flow of funds from the developing countries to the developed countries. Prices and consumption have been brought down, and it has left the African countries in such a situation that they are no longer such strong trading partners as before. Look at the problems in such a way that the development and improvement in terms of income and human standards are kept so that both sides mutually benefit from the way the economy of the world is developing. Left with the alternative of development in our countries coming from private investment, we must be man enough to accept that we have failings and that changes of government, policies, etc. really confuse the investor. But that is not the end of the story because the conditions for investment include the exchange rate risk. We know that recently with the process of structural adjustment, the devaluation of these currencies—which were meant to be part of the package of structural adjustment—have produced effects where the earnings that are made in Nigeria when translated into foreign currency become so small that it is uninteresting to the investor. Sometimes the conditions that our countries are required to meet to attract the foreign investor change so much that you have no chance of meeting them. I do, however, accept that we ourselves create some of the problems. But you can meet all the conditions and still not attract the foreign investor because fundamentally he does not trust us. In spite of the adjustment in the Nigerian currency downward, we have not seen any foreign investment resulting from this. ECOWAS has not made progress. ECOWAS must be raised from the status of being an intergovernmental organization to making it a peoples' project. The citizens must be made aware of ECOWAS and what is going on. The European citizens are involved in the EEC and therefore they have been involved in the whole development process. If we are going to develop ECOWAS, we must do the same to involve the citizens of West Africa.

Antoine Essome

General Manager, Compagnie Financière et Industrielle, Cameroun

The process of integration in Europe is nothing new; indeed, it is something of long standing and the fact that it is being used today is probably due to the fact that the members of the Community have set themselves a deadline to complete this integration. African countries have been linked to Europe for some time. I am not too familiar with the experience of the ACP, but it seems to me that there is no reason for any real fear. Our concerns, however, should be kept in mind when European legislation is being adopted.

There was a question of Europe adopting rules on cocoa products and other oils to be added to cocoa products. The ACP countries found that if such a regulation were to be adopted, our sales to the Community would drop by several hundred thousands of tons per year. The regulation was not adopted and the rules are such that Europe now recognizes the standards prevailing in each country for this product. If our structures could explain at each stage our concern about specific problems when Europe comes to adopt certain decisions, we can make progress and make our voices heard.

But what can we contribute to the acceleration of this process of integration in Europe? I think we should introduce new concepts here. What will we continue to export—cocoa and coffee? We have talked about upgrading, better quality, but I do not think that is sufficient. For example, cocoa; we don't export a great deal, but we have found that the price paid for cocoa will be lower than the price paid for cocoa 50 years ago. If you look at the whole cocoa chain—the finished product, the chocolates have never dropped in price. We find ourselves in the part of the chain where the remuneration is very low and we are absent in the part of the chain where the price is high. So, in the future it would be wise in negotiations to reposition our production structures so that we are involved in the more remunerative parts of the production chain. This obviously means that we have to have the relevant knowledge and know-how to operate. This is where we get to the rule of the private sector. Pierre-Claver Damiba (chapter 2) said that business is really the driving force of growth. Business supplies the wealth and therefore supports development. It is the private sector that we must promote and support.

Increasingly in Europe, there seems to be no place for the African business sector to be heard and to be involved in aid. Aid goes through state structures, and they don't really represent the needs of the private sector. Perhaps the time has come for the European Community to involve the private sector more in its economic, technical, and financial cooperation. This is an important element for us. When you set up a technical project, you look for a partner and for finance as our banking structures have no funds. We would hope that we can have at least as important a role in this sector so that the Community can indeed support the private sector by involving it and by enabling it to have access to its aid mechanisms. This aid must allow production sectors to develop outside our traditional areas so that development will enable us to sell to Europe where possible but also to develop and sell to our own markets.

We need to create the conditions leading to a more propitious climate for the development of the private sector. Our present commitments to privatization are not sufficient. The state structures are no longer adequate to cater to the full involvement of the private sector.

———————◆•◆◆◆———————

Akin Mabogunje
Chairman, Pai Associates, Lagos

I raise three issues here, and they all relate to the issue of the private sector. It was Gary Busch (earlier this chapter) who talked about the private enterprises in the EEC not just as the engine but as the steering for the development. It is fair to assume that part of the reason for the failure of ECOWAS to have a direction toward a community is precisely because the private sector in those countries has not shown the same concern for one large market. One of the reasons could be that many of the major private sector enterprises in the ECOWAS region are still foreign owned, and there may be some interest in protecting their colonial turf as it were. Therefore they don't see why they should work toward one common market or if they do some of what is involved are matters of negotiation back in Europe. It doesn't necessarily involve doing very much in West Africa. You can always have a branch of Unilever in the Cote d'Ivoire or a branch of Societe Commerciale in Nigeria. However, I think it is important that we are starting to have locally based private sectors. One of the most cheering things is the better record of achievement when they started to confront the problem of the West African region.

The private sector has succeeded in establishing its own regional chamber of commerce and in starting a whole series of banks, including the ECOWAS bank, which has now opened five or six branches with headquarters in Lomé. This will hopefully make it possible for some move into the agricultural, industrial, or business field. Neither Lomé I nor Lomé II paid any attention to the private sector at all. Lomé III requested greater involvement of the private sector, and they might claim that the chamber of commerce occurred because of this. However, the reality in West Africa today is that most of the local private enterprises are small to medium size (SME), many not even in the chambers of commerce I mentioned. In a few countries like Nigeria, they have formed their own chambers of commerce because they didn't find the bigger chamber of commerce really meeting their needs. We find that if we are going to grow at all, it will not be on the basis of agriculture. It is the small-scale firms that will grow to become manufacturing enterprises. Many of them have tried to enter manufacturing with different rates of success, due to the climate, structural adjustment, etc. One of the problems is how to help expose this type of firm. They are not usually exposed, but they are going to have to be to the more rigorous technical specifications of the single market we have been talking about. Otherwise they will remain small and as the situation with the agricultural market worsens, our relation with the single market will become less and less a relevant issue. If it is going to be relevant, it must be on the basis of these new enterprises being encouraged to grow and relate to that market. Isaac Akinrele (earlier this chapter) made a suggestion that the SME of Europe may be forced to relocate in developing countries as part of their response to the increased competitiveness of the EEC itself. Another model could be that many of the small-scale African enterprises may acquire the machinery of these SMEs as they are simply rendered no longer economically operational within the new single market.

We are going to run into all sorts of problems, not just because of the obsolescence of some of the machines that belong to an older generation of technology, but spare parts and specifications, which could make their products no longer acceptable in the European market. The problem we have here goes beyond staybacks and that type of support to which a lot of interest has been directed. Increasingly, I can see agricultural produce becoming less and less of what we have to offer Europe unless we are not going to grow beyond what we are at the moment. What happens as we start to become a manufacturing area is something that we must start talking about now. One area that needs attention is the institutions of different types that we may have to start thinking about to help this relationship between ECOWAS and a single market in Europe grow and mature. It may be also that we need institutions for promoting the growth of the small- and medium-scale enterprises. Again, why doesn't the European Community think of an institution that can make it possible to direct some of the EDF funds straight to the private sector rather than through governments? I believe that this is a valid position to take.

I am aware that the issue of an ACP Trade and Investment Bank has been under discussion for some time. The ECOWAS bank is a step in the right direction. But much more needs to be done precisely because of the way in which the small enterprises are structured. There are many more things to be done in this whole area of institutional response for small- and medium-scale enterprises to the challenge of a single market. The proposed expert group should be encouraged to look at the special needs of the small- and medium-scale enterprises as they try to produce manufactured goods for the global market.

5

CONCLUSION

Olusegun Obasanjo

We have heard the European Community itself. Its objectives are to increase the power of its member states to be able to do certain things:

- To increase their ability to compete in a world that is becoming more and more competitive in economic terms.
- To survive and expand in size and available opportunities.
- To contribute effectively to world trade and the world economy and, if and when necessary, to retaliate.

Europe is eliminating physical, technical, and fiscal barriers. This is an ongoing process and has evolved step by step since 1958, both in terms of harmonization of policies and in terms of the number of European countries involved—from the Europe of six to the Europe of seven, nine, and now a Europe of 12. The process of harmonization toward a single common market continues to proceed and by the end of 1992 this process is scheduled to be completed.

The reason we in Africa and in all developing countries are talking and worrying about Europe in 1992 is because we want to know the nature of it and ensure that we are not excluded or disadvantaged by it. In the course of our deliberations, we have also come to realize that the driving or motivating factor, apart from the political will and the integrative process in Europe, is the private sector, the European companies.

When we look at 1992 itself, what are the implications? We have been told that there is no clear scientific picture of the positive and negative consequences yet. But we know that there will be consequences within Europe itself and outside Europe: the abolition of physical and technical barriers; greater opportunities and competition in a bigger market. Only those who are strong enough will be able to take advantage of increased competition. There will be no room for weaker economies in a greater single market Europe. It will encourage growth in Europe itself, which is in Europe's interest in the first instance, and in other parts of the world because there will be increased demand for their commodities, services, and goods.

If we look at the private sector investment and reinvestment, such factors as viability, commitment, investment protection, control of investment, and remission are factors that encourage investment, particularly foreign investment. But they are also necessary for local investment. There are areas and times when local investment is the forerunner of foreign investment. There are other necessary elements, factors, incentives—in terms of physical structure, i.e., transportation, communication, and in terms of security of personnel, managers, workers, and property. There are nonphysical structural incentives such as skilled manpower, information, and management. Foreign investment can aid economic development if it contributes more to national income than it extracts. But with a hospitable environment and proper incentives, direct foreign investment may be in trickles. And if it flows, it will never be a panacea nor a substitute for local investment. National and regional efforts will remain the determining factors.

There are historic, geographical, and strategic reasons for developing a special relationship between Europe and Africa. If we look at ECOWAS in particular and Africa in general, we come to the conclusion that the economic situation in Africa is more than worrying. The answer is not technical but political. Africa is being marginalized, even delinked from the rest of the world economy. If we are paying attention to Africa or West Africa or sub-Saharan Africa and Europe, that is not enough. We must look at Africa or West Africa in the context of the global economy. We must look at it beyond 1992. We must look at it today, as it is likely to be in 1992, and as it is likely to be in the year 2000. What is the hope for us?

To meet the challenges and the competition that Europe will offer in 1992, it was suggested that a regional approach and regional integration are one of the ways of seeking answers to our problems. Africa must become a block; it cannot continue for too long on the slow track of world economic development. We must see any costs that this regional approach or integration may inflict on us today in terms of future individual or collective benefits. As part of meeting this challenge we have to invest in the training of our people in all aspects of production, distribution, and marketing. We must learn the art of producing packaging, distributing, and marketing in this age. Where it is necessary to hire expertise temporarily to achieve an immediate objective, we should not be reluctant to do so. We have to create internal consumer markets as internal consumption stimulates economic activities and development. We should not really say that everything should be based on exports, we also have our internal market that should be satisfied. People must be seen as the center of whatever we do, and the human aspect of development must be taken into consideration, even in the context of the Lomé IV convention. The human dimension includes respect for fundamental human rights. There must also be an increase in our ability to process, again to increase the value added in whatever we produce and however we produce it. Although we are now talking of mainly agricultural commodities, the time has come when, in terms of diversification, we should be thinking of manufactured goods for our own consumption and for export—otherwise we will continue to be drawers of water and hewers of wood.

The issue of integration, especially in West Africa, is important. Before we can make progress in physical integration and cooperation in our subregion and in our region of Africa, we have to decarbonize ourselves mentally and be able to perceive what it is and to really conceptualize it. Other obstacles we are worried about such as political will may cease to be a problem or may be easy to deal with if we are mentally attuned to what is required and what it takes for the process of integration.

Although we have no means by which we can absolutely foresee what Europe will impose on us in 1992, judging by the objectives of its operators we are right to be apprehensive about our future relationship. We have assurances, and here at the seminar we have had these assurances repeated. We can only hope that these assurances will hold up to 1992 and beyond. What we have been told is that we don't need to have any fear about Europe of a single common market. We are told we will lose nothing in trade and aid and we must give incentives for investment in our subregion. If I may put it in my own words, we have no fear, if we shouldn't have any fear about Europe in terms of market accessibility in the completion of the single market in 1992. However, I see one great fear and that fear is the fear of inaction on our part. That fear has been there and will continue to be there unless we do something urgently about it.

About the Contributors

Olusegun Obasanjo (Nigeria), former Head of State; Chairman, Africa Leadership Forum

Alhaji Abubakar Alhaji (Nigeria), Minister for Planning and Budget

Patrick Agboh (Ghana), Expert, Secretariat of the African, Caribbean and Pacific States Group (ACP), Brussels

Isaac Akinrele (Nigeria), Director, Centre for the Development of Industry, Brussels

Martin Bangemann (Federal Republic of Germany), Commissioner and Vice-President, European Commission

Gerald Blakey (United Kingdom), Adviser to the West Africa Committee, London

Gary Busch (United States), Chairman and Managing Director, Tetraview Ltd., London and President, International Bulk Trade S.A.

Adamu Ciroma (Nigeria), former Central Bank Governor and Minister for Industries and Finance

Kenneth Dadzie (Ghana), Secretary-General of UNCTAD

Pierre-Claver Damiba (Burkina Faso), Assistant Administrator and Regional Director for Africa, UNDP

Louis Emmerij (Netherlands), President, OECD Development Centre, Paris

Antoine Essome (Cameroun), General Manager, Compagnie Financiere et Industrielle

Dieter Frisch (Federal Republic of Germany), Director-General for Development, Commission of the European Communities

Richard C. Greenhalgh (United Kingdom), Senior Member of Africa and Middle East Regional Management, Unilever, London

Adrian Hewitt (United Kingdom), Deputy Director, Overseas Development Institute, London

Edem Kodjo (Togo), Former OAU Secretary-General; President, Pan African Institute for International Relations

Carol Lancaster (United States), Fellow, Institute for International Economics, Washington D.C. and Professor, School for Foreign Service, Georgetown University

Emile van Lennep (Netherlands), Minister of State, Ministry of Finance and former OECD Secretary-General

Akin Mabogunje (Nigeria), Professor and Chairman, Pai Associates

Victor Mpoyo (Nigeria), Industrialist

Nan Nguema (Gabon), former OPEC Secretary-General

Maria de Lourdes Pintasilgo (Portugal), Member of the European Parliament and former Prime Minister

Hans d'Orville (Federal Republic of Germany), Co-ordinator, InterAction Council and Africa Leadership Forum, New York

Alassane F. Ouattara (Cote d'Ivoire), Governor, Banque Centrale des Etats de l'Afrique de l'Ouest

Mamoudou Toure (Senegal), Director, African Department, International Monetary Fund and former Minister of Economy and Finance

Kandeh Yilla (Sierra Leone), General Secretary, Sierra Leone Labour Congress